WALT WHITMAN

LIVES AND LEGACIES

———

Larzer Ziff
MARK TWAIN

David S. Reynolds
WALT WHITMAN

WALT WHITMAN

LIVES AND LEGACIES

Larzer Ziff
MARK TWAIN

David S. Reynolds
WALT WHITMAN

WALT WHITMAN

David S. Reynolds

OXFORD
UNIVERSITY PRESS

2005

OXFORD
UNIVERSITY PRESS

Oxford   New York
Auckland   Bangkok   Buenos Aires   Cape Town   Chennai
Dar es Salaam   Delhi   Hong Kong   Istanbul   Karachi   Kolkata
Kuala Lumpur   Madrid   Melbourne   Mexico City   Mumbai   Nairobi
São Paulo   Shanghai   Taipei   Tokyo   Toronto

Copyright © 2005 by David S. Reynolds

Published by Oxford University Press, Inc.
198 Madison Avenue, New York, New York 10016
www.oup.com

Oxford is a registered trademark of Oxford University Press

Library of Congress Cataloging-in-Publication Data
Reynolds, David S., 1948–
Walt Whitman / David S. Reynolds.
p. cm.
Includes bibliographical references and index.
ISBN-13: 978-0-19-517009-2
ISBN-10: 0-19-517009-1
1. Whitman, Walt, 1819–1892.
2. Whitman, Walt, 1819–1892—Knowledge and learning.
3. Literature and history—United States History—19th century.
4. Literature and society—United States History—19th century.
5. United States Civilization—19th century.
6. Poets, American—19th century—Biography.
I. Title.
PS32231.R475 2005
811'.3—dc22   2004006715

1 3 5 7 9 8 6 4 2
Printed in the United States of America
on acid-free paper

To my wife, Suzanne, and our daughter, Aline, with love

Contents

PREFACE

THE AMERICAN AUTHOR WALT WHITMAN (1819–92) CHANGED THE course of poetry. Generally recognized as the father of free verse, he liberated poetry from rhyme and meter, opening it up to the flexible rhythms of feeling and voice. Championing himself as the "bard" of American democracy, he represented in his writings the total range of experience. He was the first poet to treat sex candidly and to explore same-sex love with subtlety. Among the other distinctive features of his poetry were his all-embracing persona, his imaginative vocabulary, and his sweeping catalogs that juxtaposed crisp vignettes of people, places, and things.

The philosopher Ralph Waldo Emerson called Whitman's volume *Leaves of Grass* "the most extraordinary piece of wit and wisdom America has yet contributed," saying that it had "the best merits, namely, of fortifying and encouraging."[1] Few writers illuminate the miraculous nature of everyday life as powerfully as Whitman does. Whitman once said, "I stand for the sunny point of view—stand for the joyful conclusions."[2] "Cheer!" he declared. "Is there anything better in this world anywhere than cheer—just cheer? Any religion better?—Any art? Just cheer!" Although his verse encompassed the dark features of experience—death, insanity, loneliness, spiritual torment—it ultimately affirmed the delight and sanctity of life.

Whitman had a messianic vision of himself as the quintessential democratic poet who could help cure the many ills of his materialistic, politically fractured society. Having absorbed America, he expected America to absorb him and be mended in the process. He constantly brought attention to the historical origins of his writing. "In estimating my volumes," he wrote, "the world's current times and deeds, and their spirit, must first be profoundly estimated."[3] He described himself as a poet "attracting [the nation] body and soul to himself, hanging on its neck with incomparable love, / Plunging his seminal muscle into its merits and demerits."[4]

Drawing from the extensive research behind my cultural biography *Walt Whitman's America*, the current book is the first to describe concisely his transformation of cultural materials into poetry that never loses its power to inspire, to provoke, and to heal.

WALT WHITMAN

One

———

LIFE

WALT WHITMAN WAS BORN ON MAY 31, 1819 IN THE LONG ISLAND village of West Hills, some fifty miles east of Manhattan. He was descended from two branches of early American settlers, English on his father's side and Dutch on his mother's.

His paternal ancestors included Zechariah Whitman, who came to America from England in the 1660s and settled in Connecticut. Zechariah's son Joseph moved across the sound to an area near Huntington, Long Island, where he became a farmer and local official. He gained large land holdings that came to be known as Joseph Whitman's Great Hollow. His descendants acquired even more land and established a five-hundred-acre farm that became the Whitman family homestead. In the late eighteenth century his property was overseen by Nehemiah Whitman and his colorful wife Phoebe (better known as Sarah), who spit tobacco juice and swore liberally as she barked commands at the slaves who worked the land.

Walt Whitman's birthplace, West Hills, New York.
Library of Congress, Prints and Photographs Division

The poet's father,
Walter Whitman.
*Library of Congress, Prints
and Photographs Division*

The poet's mother,
Louisa Van Velsor Whitman.
*Library of Congress, Prints and
Photographs Division*

The Whitmans' fortunes steadily declined, and by the time the
poet's father, the carpenter and sometime farmer Walter Whitman,
had reached adulthood, only a sixty-acre parcel in West Hills remained of the family homestead. Here Walter built a sturdy frame
house in 1810, moving into it with his wife Louisa six years later.

A taciturn man with a knack for ill success and possibly a drinking problem, Walter is thought to be the subject of these famous
lines in "There Was a Child Sent Forth":

The father, strong, self-sufficient, manly, mean, anger'd, unjust,
The blow, the quick loud word, the tight bargain, the crafty lure.[1]

It is mistaken, however, to accept the common argument that the
poet resented his father and was locked in Oedipal conflict with
him. His brother George would say, "His relations with his father
were always friendly, always good."[2] The poet always remembered
with affection his father's love for children and for cattle, as well

as his carpentry skills and his sensible, freethinking attitudes toward religion.

His fondness for his father, however, did not match the intensity of his love for his mother. Louisa Van Velsor Whitman, though barely literate and sometimes hypochondriac, was imaginative, a good storyteller, and the family peacekeeper. Whitman idealized her, as in this passage:

> The mother at home quietly placing dishes on the supper-table,
> The mother with mild words, clean her cap and gown, a
>   wholesome odor falling off her person as she walks by.[3]

Louisa's ancestors had emigrated to America from Holland and had settled in Woodbury, Long Island, not far from the Whitman homestead. Her mother, Naomi ("Amy") Van Velsor, was a kindly Quaker woman whose death in 1826 was a shattering experience for the young Walt. Her father, Major Cornelius Van Velsor, was a florid, hearty farmer who often took Walt with him on his vegetable wagon when he went to sell produce in Brooklyn.

Walt was the second of eight children born to Walter and Louisa Whitman. In 1822, just before Walt turned three, his father took the growing family to live in Brooklyn, then a small village with a population of around seven thousand. Although Brooklyn was going through the building boom that by 1855 would make it the fourth largest city in America, Walter Whitman had few business talents and could not turn a profit from carpentry and real estate. His family occupied no less than seven houses in its first decade there. Of these houses Walt would write, "We occupied them, one after the other, but they were mortgaged, and we lost them."[4]

Walt would spend twenty-eight years of his life in Brooklyn, absorbing its sights and sounds. "I was bred in Brooklyn," he said later, "through many, many years; tasted its familiar life."[5] He appreciated its salubrious location between rural Long Island to the east and rapidly urbanizing Manhattan to the west, with easy access to both.

Among the Brooklyn experiences that stood out in his memory was the visit on July 4, 1825, of the great Revolutionary War hero, the Marquis de Lafayette, who came to be present at the laying of the cornerstone of a library at the intersection of Cranberry and Henry Streets. Walt, six at the time, later claimed that Lafayette had picked up several children, including himself, lifted him high and kissed him on the cheek.

There was just one public school in Brooklyn, District School No. 1 on Concord and Adams Streets. Walt attended it from 1825 (possibly earlier) until 1830. Run according to the old-fashioned Lancastrian system, which emphasized rote learning and rigid discipline, the school offered primary students a basic curriculum that included arithmetic, writing, and geography. Walt's teacher, B. B. Hallock, would recall him as "a big, good-natured lad, clumsy and slovenly in appearance." Apparently Walt was a mediocre student, since Hallock, after learning later he had become a famous writer, said, "We need never be discouraged over anyone."[6]

Walt was shaped in his youth by the liberal philosophies of deism and Quakerism. Deism, which put all religions on the same level and tried to extract from them basic moral principles, was handed down to him through his father, who had known Thomas Paine in his youth and who subscribed to the *Free Enquirer*, the radical journal edited by the deists Fanny Wright and Robert Dale Owen. The poet's mystical side owed much to the Quaker doctrine of the "inner light," by which believers received inspiration not from preachers or scriptures but from divine voices within themselves. Walt never forgot being taken at age ten to Morison's Hotel to hear the eighty-one-year-old Quaker leader Elias Hicks, a great promoter of the inner light.

Whitman left school at age eleven and had no formal schooling thereafter. His family was struggling and needed him to work to help support it. Two Brooklyn lawyers, James B. Clarke and his son Edward, hired him as an office boy. The elder Clarke got him a subscription to a circulating library that opened up the world of literature to him. He loved to pore over the novels of Sir Walter Scott, the *Arabian Nights*, and other exotic material. He stayed with the Clarkes for a year before taking on a position as a newspaper apprentice to Samuel E. Clements, editor of the Democratic weekly the *Long Island Patriot*. Clements lost his position after a scandalous lawsuit and was replaced by the paper's foreman printer, William Hartshorne. A sedate old man who had known Washington and Jefferson, Hartshorne taught Walt the rudiments of printing.

When Walt was thirteen, his parents moved back to the West Hills area of Long Island, leaving him to work in Brooklyn. He soon switched newspapers, taking a job as a compositor for the Whig *Long Island Star*, edited by Alden Spooner. He stayed with the vibrant, influential Spooner for three years before taking on a similar job in Manhattan. These printing jobs instilled in him a lifelong appreciation for the physical process of making books. He would help format and typeset the famous 1855 edition of *Leaves of Grass*, and he had a controlling hand in printing later editions of the volume. "I like to supervise the production of my books," he would say, adding that an author "might be the maker even of the body of his book—set the type, print the book on a press, put a cover on it, all with his own hands."[7]

In 1836 a tremendous fire devastated the printing district of New York, forcing Whitman to return to rural Long Island, where he became a traveling schoolteacher. He taught a basic curriculum in small one-room schoolhouses in successive villages, including Norwich, West Babylon, Smithtown, Little Bayside, and Woodbury. He used a relaxed teaching approach that contrasted with the rigid Lancastrian system of his childhood and accorded with the more liberal methods introduced in the 1830s by Bronson Alcott and Horace Mann. Instead of drilling his students, he engaged them in conversation, telling them amusing stories and asking them provocative questions. One of his students at Little Bayside, Charles A. Roe, recalled him as a personable, ruddy-faced young man who wore a black coat with a vest and black pants. Although Whitman's unconventional teaching methods delighted Roe, they exasperated a Woodbury teacher who commented that "the pupils had not gained a 'whit' of learning" under Whitman.[8]

After teaching sporadically for four years, Whitman grew tired of the classroom and the provincial students he had to deal with. Exasperated by his job in the Woodbury school, he called himself "a miserable kind of dog" and wrote a friend: "O damnation, damnation! Thy other name is school-teaching and thy residence Woodbury."[9]

Besides teaching, journalism occupied him during these years. In the spring of 1838, between teaching jobs, he founded a weekly newspaper, the *Long Islander*, which he ran out of Huntington. Not only did he serve as the paper's editor, compositor, and pressman, but also each week he did home delivery by riding his horse Nina on a thirty-mile circuit in the Huntington area.

He was no entrepreneur, however, and the exigencies of a daily schedule did not suit one who would famously write, "I lean and loafe at my ease."[10] After ten months he sold the *Long Islander*. He worked briefly as a compositor for a Manhattan newspaper and then as a typesetter for the *Long Island Democrat* in the town of Jamaica. For the latter paper he wrote "The Sun-Down Papers," a series of short prose pieces, including a didactic essay that denounced the use of tobacco, coffee, or tea, and an allegory that questioned the idea of religious certainty. While working for the *Democrat* he lived at the home of its editor, James J. Brenton, whose wife found Whitman indolent and uncouth.

Between 1841 and 1845 Whitman was in Manhattan working as a journalist and printer for various newspapers. His writings for these papers followed the conventions of popular culture. He wrote poems that used traditional rhyme and meter, short stories that ranged from the sensational to the moralistic, and a temperance novel, *Franklin Evans* (1842), which sold some twenty thousand copies, becoming his best-selling work. These early writings are not individually distinguished, but, taken together, they show him experimenting with a variety of themes he would later incorporate into his poetry.

His major journalistic stint was as the editor of the *Brooklyn Daily Eagle* from 1846 to early 1848. His many pieces for this Democratic newspaper, mainly prose sketches, manifest his fascination with the street life and cultural scene of Brooklyn and Manhattan. He also became involved in the growing controversy over slavery. A free-soil Democrat, he used the columns of the *Daily Eagle* to support the Wilmot Proviso, a proposal to prevent slavery from spreading to newly acquired western territories.

His free-soil views alienated his conservative employer, Isaac Van Anden, who fired him in January 1848. He was not long out of work. Within a few weeks he met a Southern newspaper owner,

J. E. McClure, who hired him as a clipping and rewrite man for the *New Orleans Daily Crescent*. Along with his fifteen-year-old brother Jeff, Walt traveled south by train and boat, arriving in New Orleans in late February. He was there for three months, working for the *Crescent* and tasting the exotic delights of New Orleans life. He noticed the city's octoroon women, describing them as "women with splendid bodies . . . fascinating, magnetic, sexual, ignorant, illiterate: always more than pretty—'pretty' is too weak a word to apply to them."[11] He also appears to have had a passionate relationship with a man, recorded in the first version of his poem "Once I Pass'd Through a Populous City." His time in New Orleans gave him an attraction to Southern culture, which—despite his antislavery position—never left him. As he later wrote, "O magnet-South! O glistening perfumed South! my South!"[12]

In late May, homesick and worried about the approaching yellow fever season, Walt and Jeff returned to Brooklyn via Chicago, Lakes Michigan and Erie, and the Hudson River. The slavery debate, which had intensified due to the approaching presidential election, again drew Walt's attention. He attended the great antislavery convention held in Buffalo in early August. Along with some twenty thousand others, he heard many of the era's leading antislavery orators. A month later, he founded and edited another Brooklyn newspaper, the *Daily Freeman*, designed to advance the cause of the antislavery Free-Soil Party. Like the party it supported, however, the paper was short-lived; by the following fall it was taken over by conservative Hunker Democrats.

Bitter over the unpopularity of the free-soil cause and at loose ends professionally, Whitman began scribbling vitriolic political poems. In one he excoriated weak Northern "doughfaces" who tolerated the spread of slavery. In another he sang praise to the

European revolutions of 1848, which he thought embodied a healthy working-class rebelliousness. To make ends meet, he ran a stationery shop for a time, then did carpentry work in Brooklyn. His mind, however, was not on earning a living. His brother George, who worked with him, recalled, "There was a great boom in Brooklyn in the early fifties, and he had his chance then, but you know he made nothing of that chance."[13]

Although he "made nothing" in the business sense, he was privately fashioning great literature. For years he had been jotting poetic lines in his notebook and on scraps of paper he carried with him on the bustling streets and crowded ferries in the New York area. The flowing lines came from him spontaneously, in the passion of the moment, following the loose rhythms of feeling and speech rather than the metrical patterns of traditional prosody. Later he carefully revised and arranged the lines.

Many have wondered how Whitman, who had been a dull, imitative writer of conventional poetry and pedestrian prose in the 1840s, emerged in 1855 as a marvelously innovative, experimental poet. His remarkable transformation has been attributed to a number of things, such as a mystical experience he supposedly had in the 1850s or a homosexual coming-out that allegedly liberated his imagination. In absence of reliable evidence, such explanations remain unsupported hypotheses.

Instead, it is useful to heed Whitman's own account of the origins of his poetry. "In estimating my volumes," he wrote, "the world's current times and deeds, and their spirit, must first be profoundly estimated."[14] The poet fails, he insisted, "if he does not flood himself with the immediate age as with vast oceanic tides [. . .] if he be not himself the age transfigured."[15]

Among the important influences on Whitman was the influential philosopher and lecturer Ralph Waldo Emerson. Whitman once recalled having carried in his lunch pail a volume of the philosopher's essays. He paid homage to Emerson's influence when he told the author John Townsend Trowbridge, "I was simmering, simmering, simmering; Emerson brought me to a boil."[16] Indeed, the first edition of *Leaves of Grass* has Emersonian characteristics: an emphasis on self-reliance and nonconformity; images of the miraculous beauty of the natural world; and free-flowing, prose-like lines that answered Emerson's demand for relaxed, organic poetry. Whitman also fits Emerson's description of the thoroughly democratic poet, surveying American life in its dazzling diversity.

Whitman captured this diversity to a degree that even Emerson could not have foreseen. When Emerson first read *Leaves of Grass*, he wondered about its "long foreground."[17] Whitman later would say that it was "useless to attempt reading the book without first carefully tallying that preparatory background."[18]

An important factor in that background was the slavery debate and its alarming social and political repercussions. Appalled by escalating social tensions, Whitman launched his all-inclusive poetic persona in an effort to repair a society he believed was unraveling. Under one poetic roof he gathered together disparate images from nature, city life, oratory, the performing arts, science, religion, and sexual mores. He took upon himself the messianic task of absorbing his nation, with the expectation that in turn it would absorb his poetry and be healed by its triumphant proclamation of democratic togetherness and toleration.

In 1855 Whitman gathered together poems he had written along with a hastily composed preface, supervised their printing in Brooklyn, and had them published as a broad quarto with a green jacket on which was embossed *Leaves of Grass* in gold letters. The book was unlike any poetry volume that had ever appeared in America.

Its title page included the title but not the author's name, in lieu of which appeared an engraving of the casually dressed Whitman, looking like a grizzled worker who expression and posture radiated relaxed confidence and subtle sensuality. The twelve poems in the volume were untitled. They did not look like poems but rather like rhythmic prose pieces. Their punctuation was erratic—short on commas, periods, and other normal marks, while heavily dependent on ellipses. Their content was as unconventional as their style. In his effort at democratic expansiveness, Whitman included images from every realm of experience, juxtaposing city and country, past and present, upper-class people and street types, idealism and grit, the divine and the sexual. His lines veered from crystalline clarity—"The regatta is spread on the bay . . . how the white sails sparkle!"—to presurrealistic zaniness: "I find I [. . .] am stucco'd with quadrapeds and birds all over."[19]

The result was a dazzling literary potpourri. Whitman sent a copy of his volume to Emerson, who replied that as he read it he had to rub his eyes to make certain it was a sober reality. "I have great joy in it," Emerson wrote. "I find incomparable things said incomparably well, as they must be."[20] He emphasized the fortifying, ennobling effect that Whitman had on the reader. In a soon-to-be-famous declaration, Emerson wrote, "I greet you at the beginning of a great career."

Whitman was overjoyed by Emerson's letter—so much so that he tactlessly had it reprinted in the *New York Tribune* without Emerson's permission. Whitman's enthusiasm led him to indulge in shameless self-promotion. An ex-journalist, he had connections in the press, and he decided to use them to his advantage. He wrote three long, glowing reviews of *Leaves of Grass* and had them published anonymously in friendly newspapers. In the reviews he presented himself as a totally American poet, free of European conventions, who revealed new possibilities of cultural togetherness and cohesion. "An American bard at last!" he rhapsodized about himself in a piece for the *United States Review*. "He does not separate the learned from the unlearned, the northerner from the southerner, the white from the black, or the native from the immigrant just landed at the wharf."[21]

Unfortunately, few reviewers shared Whitman's enthusiasm for *Leaves of Grass*. Although the majority of the early reviews were politely positive, none was rhapsodic, and several denounced Whitman's sexual explicitness and egotistical tone. One reviewer blasted the volume as a "mass of filth," and another insisted that its author must be "some escaped lunatic, raving in pitiable delirium."[22]

Whitman had concluded the volume's preface with the heady announcement: "The proof of the poet is that his country absorbs him as affectionately as he has absorbed it."[23] He had done his part. He had absorbed his country with thoroughness and fervor. His country, however, had failed to absorb him. To be sure, he appreciated Emerson's praise, and he was delighted when two of Emerson's distinguished friends, Henry David Thoreau and Amos Bronson Alcott, made a special trip from Concord, Massachusetts, to Brooklyn to see him.

But admiration from individuals, even eminent ones, could not satisfy a writer who had hoped his poetry would have a healing effect on American society at large. Intent on reaching the public that eluded him, he quickly prepared a second edition of his poems, published in 1856, a year after the first one had appeared. This volume, which contained twenty new poems, bringing the total to thirty-two, was in many ways different from the 1855 edition. The book was small and thick, not long and slender. Not only was each poem titled, but every title contained the word "poem" (e.g., "Poem of Walt Whitman, an American," "Poem of the Body," "Poem of Women," and so on). Unlike the first edition, this one announced itself loudly as a volume of *poems*.

Clearly Whitman was changing tack after the poor sale of the first edition in an effort to gain readers. By emphasizing the poetic content of the new edition, he may have been trying to tap into the huge audience that had been enjoyed by popular poets like Henry Wadsworth Longfellow or John Greenleaf Whittier.

At any rate, a new note of desperation had entered his writings. In his private journal he recorded having "Depressions," a feeling that "Everything I have done seems blank and suspicious" and that "people will most likely laugh at me."[24] There were dark images as well in the new poems. In "Sun-Down Poem" (later called "Crossing Brooklyn Ferry") he confessed to "dark patches" in his soul, with feelings of "guile, anger, lust, hot wishes I dared not speak, [. . .] The wolf, the snake, hog, not wanting in me."[25] In a poem eventually titled "Respondez!" he lashed out angrily at many types of authority figures—priests, reformers, teachers, and politicians—and included this telling bit of black humor about his readers: "Let him who is without my poems be assassinated!"[26] As for the line about his country absorbing him, he now included it in a poem (later "By Blue Ontario's Shore") in which he made a significant addition: "The proof of a poet shall be *sternly deferr'd* till his country absorbs him as affectionately as he has absorb'd it" [author's italics].[27]

His zeal to be popularly approved was also evidenced by the physical format of the 1856 edition. Without asking Emerson, he printed the philosopher's statement "I greet you at the beginning of a great career" on the spine of the book in gold lettering. Also without permission, as after matter to the volume he printed Emerson's entire letter and even included a long letter responding to his "Dear Master" in which he predicted that soon "the average annual call for my Poems is ten or twenty thousand copies—more, quite likely."[28]

The prediction proved wildly inaccurate. The 1856 edition was an even less popular than the first one had been. Although Whitman continued—even accelerated—his writing of poetry, his attention drifted to other ways of reaching the public. He fantasized about becoming what he called a "wander-speaker," traveling from place to place and delivering his social message directly to Americans. His aim was "*always to hold the ear of the people.*"[29] He wrote articles on many aspects of current life for local newspapers and apparently edited the Brooklyn *Daily Times* in 1856–1857.

He had become something of a social dropout. He now dressed like a bohemian artist, with shaggy hair and a gray beard, and wearing a striped calico jacket over a red flannel shirt and coarse overalls. The late 1850s found him frequenting Pfaff's, an underground saloon on Broadway in Manhattan. There he shared drinks and conversation with a group of colorful people: the owner Charles Pfaff, a poet and Abolitionist; the actress Ada Clare, notorious for her many lovers and her risqué stage roles; the author Fitz-Hugh Ludlow, whose book *The Hasheesh Eater* was a pioneering account of the psychedelic drug experience; Bram Stoker, the Poe-like writer of Gothic tales; and many others, including the young William Dean Howells.

His personal life was turbulent. He appeared to have had a brief affair with a woman, possibly Ada Clare. His journals are full of brief descriptions of men he had met and befriended. He wrote a poetry sequence, to be titled "Live Oak with Moss," that evidently describes the joys and pains of an intense but ill-fated relationship with a man. This sequence would be integrated into the "Calamus" cluster of the 1860 edition of *Leaves of Grass*, which was about same-sex love.

This third edition was formatted differently from the first two, suggesting that Whitman was trying still another tactic to achieve a wide readership. The edition came about when a Boston publishing firm run by William Thayer and Charles Eldridge approached him with the idea. "We want to be the publishers of Walt Whitman's Poems," they wrote him. "We can and will sell a large number of copies.... Try us. You can do us good. We can do you good—pecuniarily."[30]

Whitman went to Boston in the spring of 1860, where he spent three months supervising the new edition. Whereas the first two editions had looked plebeian, this one strained for elegance. Priced high at $1.25, it was a fancy-looking volume with a decorative cover and illustrations. It was advertised as "AN ELEGANT BOOK... one of the finest specimens of modern book making."[31] It was aimed at the audience that bought pricey parlor-table books.

There were over a hundred new poems in the 1860 edition. Also, the awkward "Poem of" titles were replaced by ones that, with certain alterations, lasted over later editions. Thus, "Poem of Walt Whitman" became "Song of Myself," "Sun-Down Poem" became "Crossing Brooklyn Ferry," and so on. For the first time, Whitman organized the poems in clusters, or thematic groups, with titles that included "Sea Drift," "Children of Adam," and "Calamus." Today, the "Calamus" sequence seems the most adventurous innovation of the 1860 edition because of its frank treatment of love between men.

There was always a large amount of pain involved in his relations with his family. His father, who had struggled with poverty and perhaps alcoholism, had died in 1854. The poet was emotionally close to his mother, but she was poor, and she often complained bitterly about the travails of his siblings. Three of them—George, Jeff, and Mary—were normal enough, though they expressed little appreciation of Walt's poetry.

The others, however, were problematic, to say the least. The crippled, retarded Eddy needed constant care (for instance, he would not stop eating unless forced to). Jesse showed signs of insanity, attributed to brain damage suffered during a fall from a ship's mast. He was increasingly irrational and violent. In 1864 Walt had to commit him to the King's County Lunatic Asylum. He died six years later—reportedly of syphilis contracted from an Irish prostitute—and was buried in a pauper's field. Another brother, Andrew, was an alcoholic who contracted a throat condition, probably tuberculosis, and died in 1863. Andrew was married to a cantankerous woman, Nancy, who after his death took to the streets, had her children beg, and apparently prostituted for a time.

The most pathetic of all was Walt's sister Hannah. In 1852 she was married to an indigent Vermont artist, Charles Heyde, who turned out to be a psychotic wife-beater. In his intermittent periods of sanity he would hound Walt (himself struggling financially) for money. The long-suffering Hannah herself became unstable, assaulting her mother and Walt with letters about her horrible marriage and miserable life. Although Walt tried to maintain equanimity, he sometimes lost his temper about Hannah's husband, whom he called a snake, a cur, "the bed-buggiest man on earth."[32]

Even as he faced this stormy family situation, he had to confront the dissolution of his nation as he had known it. In 1860–1861 the Southern states seceded from the Union and formed the Confederate States of America. In 1855 Whitman had expressed a messianic mission to unify his fractured country through his loving poetic voice. In the 1860 edition of his poems he had included several verses stridently affirming national unity and brotherhood, as though he could repair national divisions by poetic fiat. He sensed, however, that the new poems would be no more effective in mending his nation than his previous ones had been. A note of skeptical self-questioning enters in some of the 1860 poems, such as "As I Ebb'd with the Ocean of Life."

When the Civil War began, though, Whitman embraced its purgative violence. To be sure, he was horrified by the physical suffering endured by soldiers on both sides of the war, which became the bloodiest war in American history, taking some 623,000 lives. Still, his sympathy for personal suffering did not preclude an enthusiasm for the war itself, which he regarded as a thunderstorm that might clear the murky political atmosphere and elicit high heroism and devotion to a larger cause from the common soldier. He had direct knowledge of the war through his brother George, who joined a New York regiment in September 1861 and spent four years fighting in many important battles. In February 1862 Walt was working as a journalist in New York when he read on a casualty list the report that "George W. Whitmore" had been wounded in the battle of Fredricksburg. Alarmed, Walt went to Washington and tracked down his brother in a nearby military camp in Alexandria, Virginia. It turned out that George had suffered a minor cheek wound and would soon return to army service.

Walt stayed on in Washington, where he got a job as a clerk in the Bureau of Indian Affairs, a division of the Department of the Interior. He spent much of his time in Washington's crowded war hospitals, where he served as a volunteer nurse. During the six years that he was in Washington, he saw over 100,000 wounded soldiers in the war hospitals. Although he would sometimes help doctors and regular nurses in their medical work, his main contribution was providing companionship and supplies to wounded soldiers. He distributed candy, fruit, oysters, stationery, and small sums of money to the soldiers. He gained a deep appreciation of the courage and devotion to a cause on the part of both Union and Confederate soldiers.

Above all, he came to admire the leader of the Union, President Abraham Lincoln. He saw Lincoln often on the streets of Washington. Whitman's intense response to Lincoln was deeply personal; Lincoln embodied everything that the 1855 persona of *Leaves of Grass* had hoped to be. He was democratic, charitable, firm, moderate, and folksy. Throughout much of the war, he was dedicated above all to preserving the American union. If in his life Lincoln was admirable to Whitman, in his death he became sacred. The assassination of Lincoln, which was witnessed firsthand by Walt's friend Peter Doyle in Washington's Ford's Theatre on April 14, 1865, was for the poet a culminating moment in American history. Lincoln's death, mourned by Southerners as well as Northerners, became an emotionally unifying event.

Whitman spent much of the rest of his life looking back on the Civil War, re-creating its mood and its scenes in poetry and lectures. Just after the war was ended, he published *Drum-Taps*, a collection of his war poems that included four poems about Lincoln as well as many others about battles, home scenes, and emotional responses to the war.

Actually, the war saved Whitman's reputation. In 1865 he was fired from his job in the Bureau of Indian Affairs by James Harlan, the Secretary of the Interior. Harlan, a stodgy Methodist, had found in Whitman's desk a copy of *Leaves of Grass*. He was outraged by its sexual imagery and dismissed Whitman on moral grounds.

As it turned out, Harlan's action contributed largely to the poet's fame. Whitman's Washington friend, the Abolitionist William Douglas O'Connor, was so enraged by the dismissal that he penned a passionate pamphlet, brilliantly titled *The Good Gray Poet*, that savaged priggish readers like Harlan and defended Whitman. O'Connor insisted that sex as treated by Whitman was

Whitman in 1887. *Ed Folsom Collection*

not scabrous but natural and pure, far removed from the pornographic literature of the day. Besides, O' Connor pointed out, Whitman had demonstrated his decency in his selfless work as a Civil War nurse.

Slowly Whitman transformed himself into what O'Connor said he was: the Good Gray Poet. The poetry he wrote after the Civil War ranged between mystical meditations on spirituality (e.g., "Passage to India," "Eidolóns"), occasional pieces (e.g., "My Canary Bird"), recollections of early life ("Paumanok"), and reflections on old age (" My 71st Year"). Gone was the all-encompassing persona of 1855 that absorbed all aspects of American life.

In Whitman's mind, Lincoln and the Civil War had obviated the need for that sweepingly democratic persona. The war, he believed, had not only restored the Union but also had proven the dignity of the American spirit—not that Whitman now idealized his nation. To the contrary, many issues he had to confront in the Reconstruction era perplexed him. He was slow to support suffrage for blacks, which caused him to split from his old friend O'Connor. He was appalled by the materialism and political corruption of post-war America, which he sharply criticized in his 1871 essay "Democratic Vistas," and he looked forward to a vague future when "a class of bards" would arise and instill in the nation a spiritual element.[33]

Three more editions of *Leaves of Grass* appeared after the Civil War: in 1867, 1871–1872, and 1881. Also published were two reprints, with some added material, in 1876 and 1892 (the so-called Deathbed Edition). The 1881 *Leaves of Grass*, published by James Osgood and Co. of Boston, is considered the most important of the new editions: in it Whitman gave his major poems their final form, placing them in sequenced clusters, often with revised punctuations and titles. With its regularized punctuation and usage, the Osgood edition is more conventional than the free-wheeling, deliberately experimental 1855 edition. Still, the 1881 *Leaves* retained most of the early poems, in all their boldness and occasional outrageousness, and added the poems Whitman had written during and after the war as well.

Whitman spent his last nineteen years living in Camden, New Jersey. A growing commercial town across the river from Philadelphia, Camden was where his brother George, now a pipe manufacturer, lived with his family. The poet had come to Camden in 1873 to be with his mother, who was dying. Her death was a crushing blow to him. Around the time of her death, Walt suffered a stroke that left him partly paralyzed in a leg. Thenceforth he needed a cane—and later, after several more strokes, a wheelchair—to move around.

Still, he remained active as a writer and lecturer. His fame grew steadily. He was venerated by a number of British writers, who prepared the way for his growing acceptance by his native country. His poetry moved the English woman Anne Gilchrist so deeply that she moved to America in 1876 to offer herself to him. Since his main romantic interest remained young men, he did not have a love affair with her, but he befriended her when she settled in Philadelphia.

In 1882 Whitman bought his own home in Camden, a narrow, two-story frame house on Mickle Street. Many people came to see the now-famous Good Gray Poet, including Oscar Wilde, Edmund Gosse, and Thomas Eakins, who painted his portrait. His last four years were ones of physical debility brought on by strokes and tuberculosis. During these years, he spoke almost daily with the young radical Horace Traubel, who took extensive notes on the conversations, which were later printed as the multivolume *With Walt Whitman in Camden*. In early 1892 Whitman began to fail. He died in his Mickle Street home on March 26, 1892 and was buried in Camden's Harleigh Cemetery under a stone that simply says "Walt Whitman." He had arranged earlier to have the bodies of his parents and four siblings moved there as well.

Horace Traubel, who visited Whitman almost daily from 1888 to 1892, making voluminous records of the poet's conversations.
Library of Congress, Prints and Photographs Division

Two

POPULAR CULTURE, CITY LIFE, AND POLITICS

"Remember," Whitman once said, "the book [*Leaves of Grass*] arose out of my life in Brooklyn and New York from 1838 to 1853, absorbing a million people, for fifteen years, with an intimacy, an eagerness, an abandon, probably never equalled."[1] He produced what he called "the idiomatic book of my land" by listening attentively to his land's many idioms.[2]

As the ultimate democrat, Whitman wanted his verse to reflect popular tastes, urban experience, and democratic politics. At the same time, he saw clearly the deficiencies of each. Poetry was Whitman's way of *transforming* images from everyday life so that readers would discover America's highest potential. If, as he once said, his poetry was "a great mirror or reflector" of society, it was a mirror in which America saw itself artistically improved.

Before producing the 1855 *Leaves of Grass*, Whitman had been immersed for over a dozen years in the rough-and-tumble world of New York journalism. As a writer and an editor for various

Manhattan and Brooklyn newspapers, he had participated in the cultural life of these cities.

The temperance movement, for example, was a rich source of imagery to him. Responding to the astounding rate of alcohol consumption in America, the Washingtonian temperance movement arose during the early 1840s. Whitman wrote a number of temperance works as a young journalist. The longest, the novel *Franklin Evans* (1842), has no less than four different plots that illustrate the dire effects of alcohol on family life. The most popular work that Whitman wrote during his lifetime, *Franklin Evans*, issued in cheap format as a twelve-cent pamphlet novel, sold some twenty thousand copies. It was, in Whitman's italicized words, "written *for the mass*."[3]

How serious was Whitman about temperance? In old age he dismissed *Franklin Evans* as "damned rot—rot of the very worst sort" and joked that he wrote it in three days while he was drunk.[4] Still, temperance had a formative influence on him. He knew the damage excessive drinking could cause by witnessing his own family— probably his father and certainly his brother Andrew. Whitman himself was only a moderate drinker for most of his life.

He imported the images and attitudes of temperance into his poetry, associating drunkards with impure or disgusting things. "A drunkard's breath," he wrote in "A Hand-Mirror"; "unwholesome eater's face, venerealee's flesh, / Lungs rotting away piecemeal, stomach sour and cankerous, / Joints rheumatic, bowels clogged with abomination."[5] In "Song of the Open Road" he declared that "no rumdrinker or venereal taint is permitted here."

He also transformed imagery from another popular genre of his time: sensational literature. During the 1830s and '40s a revolution in print technology occurred. The cheaply produced penny newspaper, replacing the stodgy six-penny newspaper of the past, featured a new kind of journalism that was populist, readable, and, above all, sensational. More printing advances brought inexpensive pamphlet novels that were hawked on streets and in railway stations. Popular writers of pulp novels such as George Lippard, Joseph Holt Ingraham, and George Thompson tried to outdo each other in the amount of sex and gore they could put into their novels, many of which dripped with blood.

Whitman was aware of the growing popularity of sensational literature. As a young journalist, he wrote sensational poems and stories for newspapers. Among them was "The Inca's Daughter," in which an Inca maid is tortured on the rack and then stabs herself with a poisoned arrow; "The Spanish Lady," whose aristocratic heroine is stabbed by "one whose trade is blood and crime";[6] and "Richard Parker's Widow," in which a maddened woman disinters her executed husband's coffin and embraces the corpse. In the newspapers he edited, he sometimes catered to popular taste by printing horrid accounts of crimes and accidents.

In a newspaper article he noted the great popularity of "blood and thunder romances with alliterative titles and plots of startling interest," written for the many readers who "require strong contrasts, broad effects and the fiercest kind of 'intense' writing generally." He conceded that such writing was "a power in the land, not without great significance in its way, and very deserving of more careful consideration than has hitherto been accorded it."[7]

A power in the land indeed, but, he finally decided, *not* a power for good. He eventually recognized the limitations of these narratives, which he believed had little redeeming literary or moral value. To counteract what he saw as the deleterious effects of popular sensational literature he included in his poems sensational images—

such as a tale of a bloody battle in Texas followed by one of a skirmish at sea in "Song of Myself"[8]— that gained dignity when rendered in Whitman's flowing, biblical rhythms and when juxtaposed with refreshing nature images.

A similarly ameliorative strategy governs his treatment of city life in *Leaves of Grass*. Whitman lived in a period of rapid urbanization. The American city as he knew it was in many respects disagreeable. In the days before asphalt, the ill-lit streets of Manhattan were mostly unpaved. As Whitman often complained, they became mud sinks in the winter and dust bowls in the summer. Since sewage was primitive, garbage and slops were tossed into the streets, providing a feast for roaming hogs, then the most effective means of waste disposal. Cows were regularly herded up public avenues to graze in outlying farm areas. Since police forces were not yet well organized, the crime rate was high in Manhattan, which Whitman called "one of the most crime-haunted and dangerous cities in all of Christendom."[9]

Whitman complained in newspaper articles that even his relatively clean home city, Brooklyn, had problems similar to Manhattan's. Since the city's drinking water still came from public pumps, Whitman feared Brooklynites were being slowly poisoned:

> Imagine all the accumulations of filth in a great city—not merely the slops and rottenness thrown in the streets and byways, . . . but the numberless privies, cess-pools, sinks and gulches of abomination— . . . the unnameable and unmeasurable dirt that is ever, ever filtered into the earth through its myriad pores, and which as surely finds its way into the neighborhood pump-water, as that a drop of poison put in one part of the vascular system, gets into the whole system.[10]

As for street animals, Brooklyn featured an even greater variety than Manhattan, since it was a thoroughfare to the farms on nearby Long Island. The problem provoked this outburst by Whitman in the *Brooklyn Evening Star*: "Our city is literally overrun with *swine*, outraging all decency, and foraging upon every species of eatables within their reach. . . . Hogs, Dogs and Cows should be banished from our streets."[11]

The city that appears in Whitman's poetry is not the squalid, perilous place he lamented in his journalism. In his most famous urban poem, "Crossing Brooklyn Ferry," he views both Brooklyn and Manhattan from the improving distance of a ferryboat that runs between them. The poem cleanses the city through distancing and through refreshing nature imagery. Manhattan is not the filthy, chaotic "Gomorrah" of Whitman's journalism but rather "stately and admirable . . . mast-hemm'd Manhattan."[12] Brooklyn is not the hog-infested, crowded city of his editorials but rather the city of "beautiful hills" viewed from the sparkling river on a sunlit afternoon.

If in his journalism he often lamented the city's filth and crime, in "Song of Myself" he turned to its dazzle and show: "The blab of the pave, tires of carts, sluff of boot-soles, talk of the promenaders." In his poetry he called New York City "Mannahatta," an ennobling Native American word that he called a "choice aboriginal name, with marvelous beauty, meaning." His poem "Mannahatta" delectates in the name while it minimizes less admirable features of the city.

Just as he poeticized the city, so he improved upon the denizens of the city streets. He presented flattering portraits of two types of urban males: the "b'hoy" (or "Bowery Boy"), and the "rough." When Whitman in "Song of Myself" describes himself as "Turbulent, fleshy, sensual, eating, drinking, and breeding," he is not giving an accurate account of himself. In real life, Whitman was, ordinarily, placid. He was not known for overindulgence in "eating, drinking." As for "breeding," he did not have children.

If the persona's unrestrained machismo says little about Whitman, it says a lot about the roistering types he observed on city streets. The "b'hoy" was typically a butcher or other worker who spent after-hours running to fires with engines, going on target excursions, or promenading on the Bowery with his "g'hal." The b'hoy clipped his hair short in back, kept his long sidelocks heavily greased with soap (hence his sobriquet "soap-locks"), and perched a stovepipe hat jauntily on his head. He always had a cigar or chaw of tobacco in his mouth. When featured as a character in popular plays and novels as "Mose" or "Sikesey," the b'hoy became a larger-than-life American figure who was irrepressibly pugnacious and given to violent escapades.

As a New Yorker who fraternized with common people, Whitman mingled with the workers who made up the b'hoy population. He later recalled going to plays on the Bowery, and "the young ship-builders, cartmen, butchers, firemen (the old-time 'soap-lock' or exaggerated 'Mose' or 'Sikesey,' of Chanfrau's plays,) they, too, were always to be seen in these audiences, racy of the East River and the Dry Dock."[13] In his book on language, *An American Primer*, he recorded several slang expressions used by "the New York Bowery Boy" and praised "the splendid and rugged characters that are forming among these states, or have already formed,— in the cities, the firemen of Mannahatta, and the target excursionist, and Bowery Boy."[14]

One of his goals as a poet was to capture the vitality and defiance of the b'hoy:

> The boy I love, the same becomes a man not through derived
>   power, but in his own right,
> Wicked rather than virtuous out of conformity or fear,
> Fond of his sweetheart, relishing well his steak,
> Unrequited love or a slight cutting him worse than sharp steel
>   cuts,
> First-rate to ride, to fight, to hit the bull's eye, to sail a skiff,
>   to sing a song or play on the banjo,
> Preferring scars and the beard and faces pitted with smallpox
>   over all latherers,
> And those well-tann'd to those that keep out of the sun.[15]

His whole persona in *Leaves of Grass*—wicked rather than conventionally virtuous, free, smart, prone to slang and vigorous outbursts—reflects the b'hoy culture. One early reviewer opined that his poems reflected "the extravagance, coarseness, and general 'loudness' of Bowery boys," with also their candor and acceptance of the body. Another generalized, "He is the 'Bowery Bhoy' in literature."[16]

Another street group Whitman watched with interest was variously called the "roughs," "rowdies," or "loafers," a distinct class of gang members and street loungers who roved through Manhattan's poorer districts and often instigated riots. Rival companies of roughs formed gangs with names like the Plug Uglies, the Roach Guards, the Shirt Tails, the Dead Rabbits.

Whitman's poems presented an improved version of street types whose tendencies to violence and vulgarity he frowned upon. "Mobs and murderers appear to rule the hour," he wrote in 1857 in the Brooklyn *Daily Times*. "The revolver rules, the revolver is triumphant."[17] "Rowdyism Rampant" was the title of an alarmed piece in which he denounced the "law-defying loafers who make the fights, and disturb the public peace"; he prophesied that "some day decent folks will take the matter into their own hands and put down, with a strong will, this rum-swilling, rampant set of rowdies and roughs."[18]

He presented an improved version of rowdies and loafers in his poetry. "Already a nonchalant breed, silently emerging, appears on the streets," he wrote in one poem, describing the type in another poem as "Arrogant, masculine, naive, rowdyish / [...] Attitudes lithe and erect, costume free, neck open, of slow movement on foot."[19] In a draft of another poem he wrote that he alone sang "the young man of Mannahatta, the celebrated rough."[20]

Early reviewers of *Leaves of Grass* saw the link between the poet and New York street culture. The very first review placed Whitman in the "class of society sometimes irreverently styled 'loafers.'"[21] The second review likewise called Whitman "a perfect loafer, though a thoughtful, amiable, able one."[22] The decorous James Russell Lowell declared, "Whitman is a rowdy, a New York tough, a loafer, a frequenter of low places, a friend of cab drivers!"[23]

Some, however, realized that Whitman was a rough with a difference. Charles Eliot Norton called him in a review "a compound of New England transcendentalist and New York rowdy."[24] Those who saw Whitman's infusion of a philosophical, contemplative element into street types accurately gauged his poetic purpose. Appalled by squalid forms of urban loafing, he outlined new forms of loafing in his poems. "Walt Whitman, an American, one of the roughs, a kosmos"—this famous self-description in "Song of Myself" uplifts the rough by placing him between words that radiate patriotism ("an American") and mysticism ("a kosmos").[25] Purposely in his poems Whitman shuttled back and forth between the grimy and the spiritual with the aim of cleansing the quotidian types that sometimes disturbed him.

The same recuperative process that governed his poetic treatment of popular literature and city life characterized his depiction of politics. His reaction to what he regarded as the American government's abysmal failure to deal with key social problems was a driving force behind his poetry. He deployed his poetic persona to heal a nation he thought was on the verge of coming apart.

"Of all nations," Whitman wrote in 1855, "the United States ... most need poets."[26] America needed poets because, he believed, it failed to live up to its own ideals. It preached human equality but held more than three million African Americans in bondage. It stood for justice but treated the poor and the marginalized unjustly. It endorsed tolerance but discriminated against people of different ethnicities and religions. It was a democracy, but rampant corruption often negated the votes of the people.

There was a strong impulse in Whitman to lash out against America, for he saw himself as a literary agitator. He once declared, "I think agitation is the most important factor of all—the most deeply important. To stir, to question, to suspect, to examine, to denounce!"[27] In the 1855 preface to *Leaves of Grass* he announced that in a morally slothful age the poet is best equipped to "make every word he speaks draw blood ... he never stagnates."[28]

Key lines in his poems echo this zestful tone: "I am he who walks the States with a barb'd tongue, questioning every one I meet"; "Let others praise eminent men and hold up peace, I hold up agitation and conflict."[29]

He was responding to very real social problems. Class divisions were growing at an alarming rate. Whitman, whose family felt the constant pinch of poverty, lamented this economic inequality in his poetry. He could sound like Karl Marx or George Lippard when he depicted the grotesque rich: "I see an aristocrat / I see a smoucher grabbing the good dishes exclusively to himself and grinning at the starvation of others as if it were funny, / I gaze on the greedy hog."[30] In "Song of Myself" he repeated the charge often made by labor reformers that the "idle" rich cruelly appropriated the products of the hard-working poor:

> Many sweating, ploughing, thrashing, and then the chaff for
>   payment receiving,
> A few idly owning, and they the wheat continually claiming.

The 1850s was also a decade of unprecedented political corruption, a time of vote-buying, wire-pulling, graft, and patronage on all levels of state and national government. There was historical reference, then, for Whitman's venomous diatribes, as in the 1855 preface where he impugned the "swarms of cringers, suckers, doughfaces, lice of politics, planners of sly involutions for their own preferment to city offices or state legislatures or the judiciary or congress or the presidency."[31]

The chaos created by the slavery debate caused the collapse of the old party system. He wrote that the parties had become "empty flesh, putrid mouths, mumbling and squeaking the tones of these conventions, the politicians standing back in the shadow, telling lies." Those responsible for selecting America's leaders came "from political hearses, and from the coffins inside, and from the shrouds inside the coffins; from the tumors and abscesses of the land; from the skeletons and skulls in the vaults of the federal almshouses; from the running sores of the great cities."

Whitman's wrath against governmental authority figures extended to presidents. The administrations of Millard Fillmore, Franklin Pierce, and James Buchanan eroded his confidence in the executive office because of these leaders' compromises on the slavery issue. Whitman branded these three presidencies before Lincoln as "our topmost warning and shame," saying they illustrated "how the weakness and wickedness of rulers are just as eligible here in America under republican, as in Europe under dynastic influences." In "The Eighteenth Presidency!" he lambasted Pierce in scatological metaphors: "The President eats dirt and excrement for his daily meals, likes it, and tries to force it on The States. The cushions of the Presidency are nothing but filth and blood. The pavements of Congress are also bloody."

Whitman was so critical of public figures that one might think that the final effect of his writing was bleak or negative. Quite the opposite, however, was true. It was precisely because of his disillusion with what America had become that he tried mightily to depict an alternative America in his poetry. *Leaves of Grass* was his democratic utopia. It presented a transfigured America, one that *truly* lived up to its ideals of equality and justice. It was America viewed with an intense, willed optimism.

For all his severe words about his nation's shortcomings, Whitman did not join any of the radical reforms—Abolitionism, women's rights, working-class reform, the free love movement, and others—that were the main vehicles of social protest in his era. He had a conservative side. He loved to say: "Be radical, be radical, be radical—be not too damned radical."[32] He once confessed, "I am somehow afraid of agitators, though I believe in agitation."

He feared what then was called "ultraism," or any form of extreme social activism that threatened to rip apart the social fabric. His ambivalence toward Abolitionism was especially revelatory.

On the one hand, he hated slavery and wished to see it abolished. During the 1840s he joined the so-called Barnburners, the antislavery wing of the Democratic Party. In his newspaper columns he vigorously protested against the proposed extension of slavery into western territories conquered during the Mexican War. In the 1848 election he worked for the Free-Soil Party, and in the early fifties his favorite politician was John P. Hale, the dynamic antislavery senator from New Hampshire.

At the same time, Whitman could not tolerate Abolitionism as it was advocated by the era's leading antislavery reformer, William Lloyd Garrison. He thought that Garrison went too far in his attacks on American institutions. Garrison condemned the Constitution as "a covenant with death and a compact with hell" because of its implicit support of slavery. His battle cry, "No union with slaveholders!" reflected his conviction that the North should immediate separate from the slaveholding South.

Whitman, who prized the Constitution and the Union, called the Abolitionists "foolish red-hot fanatics," an "angry-voiced and silly set."[33] He hated the nullification doctrines of Southern fire-eaters as much as he did the disunionism of the Garrisonians. He explained, "Despising and condemning the dangerous and fanatical insanity of 'Abolitionism'—as impracticable as it is wild—the Brooklyn *Eagle* just as much condemns the other extreme from that." [34]

His mixed feelings about the antislavery movement were also reflected in his middling position on the Fugitive Slave Law of 1850. On the one hand, he excoriated the law's supporters in his poems "Blood-Money," "Wounded in the House of Friends," and "A Boston Ballad."

At the same time, he believed that fugitive slaves must be returned to their owners. "MUST RUNAWAY SLAVES BE DELIVERED BACK?" he asked in "The Eighteenth Presidency!"

His answer said it all: "They must. . . . By a section of the fourth article of the Federal Constitution."[35] He called the Constitution "a perfect and entire thing, . . . the grandest piece of moral machinery ever constructed" whose "architects were some mighty prophets and gods." He valued the Constitution so highly that he was willing to support its directive that fugitives from labor must be returned.

His views were similar to Abraham Lincoln's, then a little-known Illinois lawyer and ex-congressman. Though morally opposed to slavery, Lincoln, like Whitman, hated Abolitionism because he put a high premium on the Union. He also supported the return of fugitive slaves because the Constitution demanded it.

Fearing extremes, Whitman began tentatively testing out statements that balanced opposite views, as though rhetorical juxtaposition would dissolve social tensions.

His earliest jottings in his characteristic prose-like verse showed him attempting to balance antislavery and proslavery views in poetry. Fearing above all a separation of the Union, he penned lines in which an imagined "I" identified lovingly with both sides of the slavery divide:

I am the poet of slaves and of the masters of slaves, [. . .]
I go with the slaves of the earth equally with the masters
And I will stand between the masters and the slaves.[36]

Hoping to defend the Union while at the same time making room for the South's demand for states rights, he listed among "Principles We Fight For" the following:

The freedom, sovereignty, and independence of the respective
    States.
The Union—a confederacy, compact, neither a consolidation,
    nor a centralization.[37]

When he wrote these words in 1846, he could not know that fifteen years later America itself would be divided between the Union, representing federal power, and the Confederacy, representing states rights. But he did see that the issue was one of momentous importance, at the absolute heart of American life. In a prose work he said that one of his main poetic objectives from the start was to solve "the problem of two sets of rights," those of "individual State prerogatives" and "the national identity power—the sovereign Union." [38]

He shied away from movements that seemed to upset that delicate balance, and he tried mightily to restore that balance in his poetry. On this theme, the message of his poems was clear: balance and equipoise by poetic fiat. The poet was to be the balancer or equalizer of his land. "He is the arbiter of the diverse and he is the key," Whitman emphasized in the 1855 preface to *Leaves of Grass*. "He is the equalizer of his age and land . . . he supplies what wants supplying and checks what wants checking."[39]

Seeing that the Union was imperiled by Northern Abolitionists and Southern fire-eaters, in the 1855 preface he affirmed "the union always surrounded by blatherers and always calm and impregnable." The President would no longer be the people's referee; now the poet would be. The genius of the United States, he wrote, was not in presidents or legislatures but "always most in the common people," as it was better to be a poor free laborer or farmer than "a bound booby and rogue in office." His early poems are full of long catalogs of average people at work.

The basic problem of the conflicting rights of the individual and the mass was resolved imaginatively in the ringing opening lines of the first edition:

I celebrate myself,

And what I assume you shall assume,

For every atom belonging to me as good belongs to you.

These lines radiated intense individualism and, simultaneously, intense democracy. The "I" celebrates himself but also announces his complete equality with others—the "you." Whitman announces to us that this individual-versus-mass tension can be resolved not by arguments over states rights and nationalism but by reference to something much larger: the physical operations of nature, "For every atom belonging to me as good belongs to you." All humans occupy the same physical world. They share atoms. There is a fundamental democracy in nature itself. Indeed, nature becomes a key unifying factor for Whitman. His title, *Leaves of Grass*, referred not only to the "leaves" (pages) of his volume but also to the earth's most basic form of vegetation—grass. Metaphorically, grass resolved the issue of individualism versus the mass. It was comprised of individual sprouts that could be admired on their own, as Whitman's persona does when he declares, "I lean and loafe at my ease observing a spear of summer grass." Also, grass was the earth's ultimate symbol of democracy and human togetherness, for it grew everywhere. As Whitman writes, "Sprouting alike in broad zones and narrow zones, / Growing among black folks as among white, / Kanuk, Tukahoe, Congressman, Cuff, I give them the same, I receive them the same."

He knew that Southerners and Northerners were virtually at each others' throats, so he made a point in his poems constantly to link the opposing groups. He proclaimed himself "A Southerner soon as a Northerner, a planter nonchalant and hospitable down by the Oconee I live, / [. . .]At home on the hills of Vermont or in the woods of Maine, or the Texan ranch." When he addressed the issues of sectionalism and slavery in his poetry, he also struck a middle ground. In the 1855 preface he assures his readers that the American poet shall "not be for the eastern states more than the western or the northern states more than the southern." He writes of "slavery and the tremulous spreading hands to protect it, and the stern opposition to it which shall never cease till it ceases of the speaking of tongues and the moving of lips cease." The first half of this statement gently embraces the Southern view; the second half airs sharp antislavery anger but leaves open the possibility that it may be a very long time before slavery disappears.

Fearing the sectional controversies that threatened disunion, Whitman represented the Southern point of view in his poetry, as when he described a plantation: "There are the negroes at work in good health, the ground in all directions is cover'd with pine straw." At the same time, however, his view was close to that of antislavery activists of the 1850s who were emphasizing the humanity of African Americans. He takes a radically humanitarian view toward blacks several times in the 1855 edition. The opening poem, later titled "Song of Myself," contains a long passage in which the "I" takes an escaped slave into his house and washes and feeds him, keeping his rifle ready at the door to fend of possible pursuers. In another passage he actually becomes "the hounded slave," with dogs and men in bloody pursuit. In a third he admires a magnificent black driver, climbing up with him and driving alongside of him. "I Sing the Body Electric" presents a profoundly humanistic variation on the slave auction, as the "I" boasts how humanly valuable his slave is: "There swells and jets a heart, there all passions, desires, reachings, aspirations, / [...]In him the start of populous states and rich republics."

Such passages help explain why his poetry has won favor among African American readers. The ex-slave and Abolitionist lecturer Sojourner Truth was rapturous in her praise of *Leaves of Grass*. The Harlem Renaissance writer Langston Hughes could talk of Whitman's "sympathy for Negro people," and June Jordan said, "I too am a descendant of Walt Whitman."[40]

Whitman's growing disillusion with authority figures sparked his deep faith in common people and in the power of populist poetry. America, he believed, desperately needed a poet to hold together a society that was on the verge of unraveling. He created his powerful, all-absorbing poetic "I" to heal a fragmented nation that, he hoped, would find in his poetry new possibilities for inspiration and togetherness. With almost messianic expectations for the impact of his writings, Walt Whitman believed that America would reverse its downward course by seeing its diverse cultural and social materials reflected in the improving mirror of democratic poetry.

Three

THEATER, ORATORY, AND MUSIC

WHEN WHITMAN SAID HE SPENT HIS YOUNG MANHOOD "ABSORBING theatres at every pore" and seeing "everything, high, low, middling," he revealed his complete identification with the performance culture of antebellum America.[1]

There was a fine line in antebellum theaters between enthusiastic applause and uncontrolled mob frenzy. The b'hoys and roughs of the gallery went to the theater as much to engage in deviltry as to see plays. Often the din of clapping, yelling, cheering, or hissing drowned out the actors. At the slightest provocation, unruly elements in the audience would throw things onto the stage. Whitman fondly recalled "those long-kept-up tempests of hand-clapping peculiar to the Bowery—no dainty kid-gloved business, but electric force and muscle from perhaps 2,000 full-sinew'd men."[2]

Actors reciprocated in kind through an intense kind of emotionalism that defined the "American" acting style. The greatest exponent of this style was Junius Brutus Booth, Whitman's favorite actor and the leading tragedian of antebellum America. "His genius," said Whitman, "was to me one of the grandest revelations of my life, a lesson of artistic expression." "He had much to do with shaping me in those early years," he added. The neurotic but talented Booth was for Whitman an inspired genius who defied convention and established a new style. Whitman declared that "he stood out 'himself alone' in many respects beyond any of his kind on record, and with effects and ways that broke through all rules and all traditions."

The aspect of Booth that most impressed Whitman was his powerful expression. "I demand that my whole emotional nature be powerfully stirred," Whitman generalized about acting.[3] No one could satisfy this craving more than Booth, who was a key figure in the development of the new acting style. Whitman explained, "The words fire, energy, *abandon*, found in him unprecedented meanings."[4] It was the peaks for which he became known. "When he was in a passion," Whitman wrote, "face, neck, hands, would be suffused, his eye would be frightful—his whole mien enough to scare audience, actors; often the actors *were* afraid of him."[5]

When Whitman said Junius Brutus Booth shaped him in his early years, he was referring to the fervent emotionalism that made Booth seem not an actor but a real person. As Whitman put it, Booth "not only seized and awed the crowded house, but all the performers, without exception."[6] Booth evidently crossed the line between acting and real life. Many times while playing Othello he became so involved in the role that other actors had to pull him away lest he actually kill the Desdemona of the night. As the sword-wielding Richard III, he was known to pursue Richmond out of the theater and continue fighting on the street.

In several senses, Whitman himself was an actor, in daily life and in his poetry. "I have always had a good deal to do with actors: met many, high and low," he said.[7] Obviously they shared trade secrets with him. Not only did he declaim passages from plays on the streets and at the seashore, but he took pride in subtleties of interpretation. Thomas A. Gere, an East River ferry captain, recalled that he would regale passengers with Shakespearian soliloquies, stop himself in the middle and say "No! no! no! that's the way bad actors would do it," and then begin again. "In my judgment," Gere said, "few could excel his reading of stirring poems and brilliant Shakespearian passages."[8] His "spouting" of loud Shakespeare passages on the New York omnibuses reflected his participation in the zestful turbulence of American life.

He developed a theatrical style in his daily behavior. When he grew his beard and adopted his distinctive casual dress in the 1850s, people on the street, intrigued by his unusual appearance, tried to guess who he might be: Was he a sea captain? A smuggler? A clergyman? A slave trader? One of his friends called him "a poseur of truly colossal proportions, one to whom playing a part had long before become so habitual that he ceased to be conscious that he was doing it." [9]

Nowhere did he act so much as in his poetry. The "I" of *Leaves of Grass* has proved puzzling to critics. Some have seen it as a sublimation of private anxieties and desires. Others see it as a complete fiction, with little reference to the real Whitman, as indicated by the many differences between the poetic persona and the man. Such confusions can be partly resolved by recognizing that the "real" Whitman, as part of a participatory culture, was to a large degree an actor, and that his poetry was his grandest stage, the locus of his most creative performances. When developing his poetic persona in his notebooks, he compared himself to an actor on stage, with "all things and all other beings as an audience at a play-house perpetually and perpetually calling me out from behind the curtain." In the poem "Out from Behind this Mask" he calls life "this drama of the whole" and extends the stage metaphor by describing "This common curtain of the face contain'd in me for me, in you for you" and "The passionate teeming plays this curtain hid!" [10]

Few personae in literature are as flexible and adaptable as Whitman's "I." In "Song of Myself" alone he assumes scores of identities: He becomes by turns a fugitive slave, a bridegroom, a mutineer, a clock, and so on. He is proud of his role-playing ability: "I do not ask the wounded person how he feels, I myself become the wounded person"; "I become any presence or truth of humanity here." [11] Whitman is ready to absorb himself at will into many identities, regardless of gender. "I am the actor, the actress, the voter, the politician," he announces in "The Sleepers." [12] In "Crossing Brooklyn Ferry" he writes, "Live, old life! play the part that still looks back on the actor or actress, / Play the old role."

The emotional peaks of the early editions of *Leaves of Grass* seem to reflect the style of the actor he most admired, Junius Brutus Booth. Neither Booth nor Whitman was particularly demonstrative in private. But when performing—Booth on stage, Whitman in his poetry—both were volcanic. Whitman's identification with emotionally charged characters leads him to near-melodramatic peaks. "O Christ! My fit is mastering me!"; "You laggards there on guard! look to your arms! / In at the conquer'd doors they crowd! I am possess'd!"; "You villain touch! what are you doing? my breath is tight in its throat; / Unclench your floodgates, you are too much for me." [13] Like the actor who shaped him, Whitman as poetic performer took passionate expression to new heights.

Closely connected with acting was oratory, another source of Whitman's passionate voice. In old age he declared: "It has always been one of my chosen delights, from earliest boyhood up, to follow the flights particularly of American oratory."[14] As was true with the theater, his tastes in oratory were eclectic. He once wrote that he was "born, as it were, with propensities, from my earliest years, to attend popular American speech-gatherings, conventions, nominations, camp-meetings, and the like."[15]

The period from the American Revolution through the Civil War has been called the Golden Age of Oratory. The lyceum movement, which had begun in 1826 and crested in the 1850s, coordinated the appearances of lecturers in the arts, sciences, religion, philosophy, and literature. An article in Whitman's *Brooklyn Daily Times* identified the years 1853–55 as the time when "The lecture system reached its culminating point. . . . Then it was a perfect *furor*. Lectures almost usurped the place of theatres and other amusements of the kind."[16]

Whitman admired America's successful orators, whose techniques are felt in his poetry. What some have called the oratorical style of his poetry refers particularly to his "grand," rolling lines with their rhythmic repetitions and vocal inflections. There was a grandeur about serious orators like the Whig statesman Daniel Webster and the Boston lecturer Edward Everett, two he particularly admired.

Among his other favorites were the fiery antislavery politician Cassius Clay and the Brooklyn preacher Henry Ward Beecher. Clay brought a Junius Booth–like volatility to the lecture platform. Perfecting the participatory style, Clay walked back and forth as he spoke, gesticulating and emoting. Beecher regaled his huge audiences at Brooklyn's Plymouth Church with entertaining sermons that freely combined the divine and the secular—a mixture also visible in Whitman's poems, which shift quickly between the spiritual and the earthly. Beecher regularly used the first person and addressed his hearers as "you" to create a personal connection with them.

Whitman shared the interest in the new oratorical style based on audience-performer interaction. If Beecher told his hearers he was studying "you," Whitman expressed a similar eagerness to develop what he called an "animated *ego-style*" of oratory with "direct addressing *to you*."[17] If Beecher wanted his hearers to surge all around him, Whitman wrote poetry of unexampled intimacy, telling his readers:

> Come closer to me,
> Push close my lovers and take the best I possess, [...]
> I was chilled with the cold type and cylinder and wet paper
>   between us.
> I pass so poorly with paper and types.... I must pass with the
>   contact of bodies and souls.[18]

Given the high visibility of orators on the American scene, it is understandable that Whitman, who loved to test out popular fads, would try his hand at oratory. His instinct to lecture predated his instinct to write. He told Horace Traubel, "When I was much younger, way back: in the Brooklyn days— . . . I was to be an orator—to go about the country spouting my pieces, proclaiming my faith. . . . I thought I had something to say—I was afraid I would get no chance to say it through books: so I was to lecture and get myself delivered that way."[19] According to his brother George, at the peak of the lyceum craze, in the early fifties, "He wrote what his mother called 'barrels' of lectures." Although just one lecture (his March 31, 1851 address to the Brooklyn Art Union) has survived, both his notebooks and his poetry of the 1850s are filled with references to oratory. His conception of the national poet's role was related to his devotion to oratory. In his notebook he jotted this free-form reflection: "American Lectures/New sermons/America-Readings—Voices Walt Whitman's Voices."[20] The great advantage of lecturing, he saw, was direct contact with the people.

When Whitman sketched out in a notebook his own lecturing plans, he told himself to maintain verve without wildness, passion without excess. He wanted, he wrote, to develop a lecture style that was "far more direct, close, animated and fuller of live tissue and muscle than any hitherto." But he warned himself: "Be bold! be bold! be bold! Be not too bold! With all this life and on the proper emergency, vehemence, care is needed not to run into any melodramatic, Methodist Preacher, half-inebriated, political spouter, splurging modes of oratory."[21] He recoiled from undisciplined orators. As he put it, "Not hurried gabble, as the usual American speeches, lectures, &c. are, but with much breath, such precision, such indescribable meaning, slow and with interior emphasis." What was needed, then, was breadth, strength, interiority.

Actually, he was ill-equipped to be a great orator, with a voice that had range and expression but did not project well to large crowds. It was in his poetry that he presented the kind of oratorical style he had in mind. Writing for him was closely allied to speaking. One reason his poetry sounds oratorical is its air of spontaneity, of being spoken aloud. His method of composition was spontaneous. Suddenly seized with an impression or image, he would scribble it quickly on any handy scrap of paper, trying, as he explained, "to write in the gush, the throb, the flood, of the moment—to put things down without deliberation."[22] He kept separate scraps in an envelope, later bringing them together as poems after careful revision. He was never far from what he called vocalism. Of his poems he told Traubel, "I like to read them in a palpable voice: I try my poems that way—always have: read them aloud to myself."

An unsuccessful orator himself, he nonetheless gained vicarious satisfaction in experiencing the effect of that the most powerful American speakers had on their hearers:

> O the orator's joys!
> To inflate the chest, to roll the thunder of the voice out from the
>   ribs and throat,
> To make people rage, weep, hate, desire, with yourself,
> To lead America—to quell America with a great tongue.[23]

Critics have shown that the poems of the first three editions of *Leaves of Grass* are characterized by oratorical devices such as exclamations, rhetorical questions, negations, parallelism, invocations to a "you."[24] This style made some fastidious commentators uncomfortable. Rossetti, for example, found in his verse outbursts "fitted for a Yankee stump orator, but forbidden to a poet."[25] For Whitman, however, oratorical technique was a culturally accepted mode of making contact with the American public. Whitman changed the participatorial lecture style into a new participatory poetics. If the performers and speakers he admired challenged boundaries between themselves and their hearers, he tried to demolish such boundaries altogether. He coaxed, badgered, seduced the reader, reaching, as it were, right through the page.

His theory of poetry was by definition participatory and agonistic. "The reader will always have his or her part to do," he wrote, "just as much as I have mine."[26] Reading he called "a gymnast's struggle" in which the reader grapples with the author.[27] Absorbed into poetry, the antebellum personal style erased the boundary between performer and listener, between writer and reader:

Camerado, this is no book,
Who touches this touches a man.

Surveying all the entertainment experiences of his young manhood, Whitman wrote, "Perhaps my dearest amusement reminiscences are those musical ones."[28] Music was such an all-pervasive force on him that he saw himself less as a poet than as a singer or bard. "My younger life," he recalled in old age, "was so saturated with the emotions, raptures, up-lifts of such musical experiences that it would be surprising indeed if all my future work had not been colored by them."[29]

Among the titles of his poems seventy-two different musical terms appear. In the poems themselves twenty-five musical instruments are mentioned, including the violin, the piano, the banjo, the oboe, and the drums. One poem, "Proud Music of the Storm," sings praise to virtually all kinds of music, popular and classical, even mentioning by name specific operas and symphonies.

The dominant musical image group in his poetry derives from vocal music. As was true with his response to theater and oratory, he was stirred especially by what he called "the great, overwhelming, touching human voice—its throbbing, flowing, pulsing qualities." Of the 206 musical words in his poems, 123 relate specifically to vocal music, and some are used many times. "Song" appears 154 times, "sing" 117, "singing" and "singers" more than 30 times each.[30]

Whitman regarded music as a prime agent for unity and uplift in a nation whose tendencies to fragmentation and political corruption he saw clearly. Music offered a meeting place of aesthetics and egalitarianism. For all the downward tendencies he perceived among contemporary Americans, he took confidence in the shared love of music. In the 1855 preface to *Leaves of Grass* he mentioned specifically "their delight in music, the sure symptoms of manly tenderness and native elegance of soul."[31] Music allowed for sensuous release and emotional expression without the scabrousness and windy excess he saw elsewhere in popular culture. As he explained in an 1855 magazine article: "A taste for music, when widely distributed among a people, is one of the surest indications of their moral purity, amiability, and refinement. It promotes sociality, represses the grosser manifestations of the passions, and substitutes in their place all that is beautiful and artistic."[32] By becoming himself a "bard" singing poetic "songs" he hoped to tap the potential for aesthetic appreciation he saw in Americans' positive responses to their shared musical culture.

Whitman's poetic yoking of images from various cultural levels—his alternation between aria motifs and minstrel-show antics, for instance, or his combinations of high diction and slang—was reflective of the varied performance culture that surrounded him.

What Whitman especially prized was music that sprang from indigenous soil and embodied the idioms and concerns of average Americans. He discovered such music in the family singers and minstrel troupes that attained immense popularity in the mid-1840s. In a series of newspaper articles written from 1845 to 1847 Whitman rejoiced over what he saw as the distinctly American qualities of the new family singers, especially the Hutchinsons. The most popular family group before the Civil War, the Hutchinson singers consisted of three brothers—Judson, John, Asa—and their younger sister Abby, part of a talented family of thirteen boys and girls from Milford, New Hampshire. Their catchy songs ran the gamut of popular idioms, from the sentimental to the sensational, and promoted a variety of reforms, particularly temperance and antislavery. In a newspaper article titled "American Music, New and True!" (which he revised four times!) he argued that the "art music" of the foreign musicians was overly elaborate and fundamentally aristocratic, while the "heart music" of the American families was natural and democratic. Whitman wrote of the American family singers: "Simple, fresh, and beautiful, we hope no spirit of imitation will ever induce them to engraft any 'foreign airs' upon their 'native graces.' We want this sort of starting point from which to mould something new and true in American music."[33]

As an American "singer," Whitman in his poetry would strive for naturalness and what he called "a perfectly transparent, plate-glassy style, artless," characterized by "clearness, simplicity, no twistified or foggy sentences."[34] It was this kind of artlessness he saw in the Hutchinsons, whose "elegant simplicity in manner" he praised.[35]

He was powerfully stirred by the rich vocal mixtures of the singing famlies, such as the Hutchinsons' alternation between solo and group parts. He paid homage to such mixtures in his poem "That Music Always Round Me":

[N]ow the chorus I hear and am elated, [. . .]
I hear not the volumes of sound merely, I am moved by the
    exquisite meanings,
I listen to the different voices winding in and out, striving,
    contending with fiery vehemence to excel each other in
    emotion;
I do not think the performers know themselves—but now I
    think I begin to know them.[36]

Another form of American music that appealed to Whitman was the minstrel song. Particularly intriguing is the possible relationship between Whitman and the leading minstrel songwriter, Stephen Foster. Whitman commented that songs like Foster's "Old Folks at Home" were "our best work so far" in native music.[37] The first American to earn a living from songwriting, Foster first gained wide popular success in 1847 with "Oh! Susanna," followed in the next five years with "My Old Kentucky Home," "Beautiful Dreamer," "Old Dog Tray," and many others.

With the rise of Stephen Foster, American music became popular and participatory in an unprecedented way. In the days before such passive entertainments as radio and television, people would hear melodies and sing them constantly aloud to themselves, creating, as it were, their own musical programs. Whitman himself did this. Often when alone he sang popular ballads or martial songs in a low undertone, and while sauntering he hummed snatches of popular songs or operas. An East River ferryboat worker said that when passengers were few Whitman liked to regale them with "pleasant scraps and airs" in his "round, manly voice."[38]

It was Foster's music that sprang most naturally from American's lips in the early 1850s. Says the music historian Charles Hamm of Foster's impact: "Never before, and rarely since, did any music come so close to being a shared experience for so many Americans."[39]

There was ample justification, then, for Whitman's confidence that music was commonly loved and even performed by many Americans. The lines he wrote to express music's near-universal presence in American daily life was a kind of poetic gloss on the newspaper reports of the day: "I hear America singing, the varied carols I hear, / Those of mechanics, each one singing his as it should be blithe and strong"—and so forth, as he goes on to describe the singing of the mason, the boatman, the shoemaker, the wood-cutter, the wife, all "singing with open mouths their strong melodious songs."[40]

Responsive to the simple, egalitarian music of the singing families and the minstrels, Whitman was also inspired by a more sophisticated form, the opera.

He admired the great opera singers who came to America in the 1840s and '50s. He heard at least sixteen of the major singers who made their New York debuts in the next eight years, including the Italian baritone Cesare Badiali, the tenor Allesandro Bettini, the sopranos Giula Grisi and Balbina Steffanone, the contralto Marietta Alboni, and the English soprano Anna De La Grange.

Among the male singers, the ones he most admired were Badiali and Bettini. The large, broad-chested Badiali, who first appeared in New York in 1850, Whitman called "the superbest of all the superb baritones in my time—in my singing years."[41] Bettini, especially as the male lead in Donizetti's *La Favorita*, made it clear to him that art music need not be distinct from heart music. It was almost certainly Bettini to whom he paid tribute in this passage in "Song of Myself": "A tenor large and fresh as the creation fills me, / The orbic flex of his mouth is pouring and filling me full."[42] Another tenor he heard in the early fifties, Pasquale Bignole, remained so vivid a memory that upon Bignole's death in 1884 he wrote a eulogistic poem, "The Dead Tenor," reviewing by name his major operatic roles and recreating the effect of his singing:

> How much from thee! the revelation of the singing voice from thee!
> (So firm—so liquid-soft—again that tremulous, manly timbre!
> The perfect singing voice—deepest of all to me the lesson—
> trial and test of all).[43]

Among all the opera stars, the one that shone brightest for him was Marietta Alboni, the great contralto who also sang soprano roles. "For me," he told Traubel, "out of the whole list of stage deities of that period, no one meant so much to me as Alboni, as [Junius Brutus] Booth: narrowing it further, I should say Alboni alone."[44] A short, plump woman with a low forehead and black hair, Alboni had been coached in Italy by Rossini and, after several European tours, arrived in New York in the summer of 1852. Her opening on a sweltering June 23 at Metropolitan Hall was a complete triumph. "There was never a more successful concert," raved the next day's *Herald*.[45] Between that summer and the next spring in Manhattan she appeared in ten operas and gave twelve concerts of operatic selections. She also toured other cities and states. Whitman later wrote that he heard her "every time she sang in New York and vicinity."[46] "She used to sweep me away as with whirlwinds," he said.[47]

It was not Alboni's talent alone that stood out. What made her special was her combined artistry, soulfulness, and egalitarianism. A consummate artist, she was nonetheless down-to-earth and thoroughly human in her delivery. Whitman never forgot the way she got so caught up in her roles that real tears poured down her cheeks. In opera history, Alboni is remembered as one of the great representatives of *bel canto*, the flowing, simple line interrupted by vocal scrollwork that has an unearthly, almost orgasmic quality. Stylistically, it was this voluptuous, mystical aspect of her singing Whitman had in mind when he referred to her impact on his poetry. A contemporary described the effect of Alboni's *bel canto* singing: "There is an indefinable something more delicate than expression, yet akin to it, which makes her song float like a seductive aroma around her hearer, penetrating to the most delicate fi-

bres of his being, and pervading him with a dreamy delight."[48]
Whitman's verse often resonates with a *bel canto* feeling, even in
passages where music is not directly mentioned:

> Smile O voluptuous cool-breath'd earth!
> Earth of the slumbering and liquid trees!
> Earth of departed sunset—earth of the mountains misty-topt!
> Earth of the vitreous pour of the full moon just tinged with
>   blue![49]

The rapture Alboni inspired in him had more direct poetic ramifications as well. "I hear the train'd soprano (what work with hers
is this?)," he writes in "Song of Myself." "The orchestra whirls
me wider than Uranus flies, / It wrenches such ardors from me I
did not know I possess'd them." Although he included in his poems the names of several operas, opera characters, and classical
composers, he named just one singer:

> (The teeming lady comes,
> The lustrous orb, Venus contralto, the blooming mother,
> Sister of loftiest gods, Alboni's self I hear.)

As much as anything, he was intrigued by Alboni's appeal to
all classes. "All persons appreciated Alboni," he noted, "the common crowd as well as the connoisseurs." He was fascinated to see
the upper tier of theaters "packed full of New York young men,
mechanics, 'roughs,' etc., entirely oblivious of all except Alboni."[50]
In an 1855 article, "The Opera," he said of opera music: "A
new world—a liquid world—rushes like a torrent through you."
He called for an American music that might rival Europe's: "This
is art! You envy Italy, and almost become an enthusiast; you wish
an equal art here, and an equal science and style, underlain by a

perfect understanding of American realities, and the appropriateness of our national spirit and body also."[51]

An artistic music underlain by American realities. This is what he had been searching for all along in his musical experiences. In his poems he tried to forge a new kind of singing, one that highlighted American themes but also integrated operatic techniques. "Walt Whitman's method in the construction of his songs is strictly the method of the Italian Opera," he would write in 1860, and to a friend he confided, "But for the opera I could not have written *Leaves of Grass*."[52] Opera devices run through his poetry. Many of the emotionally expressive, melodic passages, such as the bird's song in "Out of the Cradle Endlessly Rocking" or the death hymn in "When Lilacs Last in the Dooryard Bloom'd," follow the slow pattern of the aria. The more expansive, conversational passages in his poetry follow the looser rhythm of the operatic recitative (Whitman once described himself "here in careless trill, I and my recitatives").[53]

To assign Whitman's poetic patterns to a single performance mode, however, is delimiting and misses the social significance of his imagery and style. In antebellum America, boundaries between different performance genres and cultural levels were permeable. Popular singers borrowed directly from the opera and from oratory. Actors and lecturers cribbed from each other. Artists in various fields mingled the high and the low. Whitman learned from them all. His verse enacted this permeability of modes. In one passage he could sound like an actor, in another an orator, in another a singer. The same was true in his daily life: He would by turns declaim, orate, sing. As both man and poet, Whitman simultaneously heard the thousand varied carols, knew the orator's joys, and played the part that looked back on the actor and actress.

Four

THE VISUAL ARTS

As with popular performance, Whitman found in photography and painting a rich mine of poetic materials. He regarded art as a means of refining and elevating the masses. In a newspaper article titled "Polishing the Common People," he called for the wide-spread distribution of artworks: "We could wish the spreading of a sort of democratical artistic atmosphere among the inhabitants of our republic."[1] His poetry was his gesture toward fostering such an artistic atmosphere.

From the new medium of photography he learned techniques of democratic realism. "In these *Leaves* [*of Grass*] everything is photographed. Nothing is poeticized," he wrote.[2] A frequenter of Manhattan daguerreotype galleries, he offered in poetry his own gallery of "photographs"—realistic vignettes of common people engaged in everyday activities.

His democratic portraits of quotidian life were also influenced by the American paintings he loved. An active member of the

Brooklyn Art Union, where he befriended many leading painters, he became so caught up in New York's art-gallery scene that he once devoted a poem, "Pictures," to describing his own head as a gallery:

> In a little house pictures I keep, many pictures hanging
>   suspended—
> It is not a fixed house,
> It is round—it is but a few inches from one side of it to the
>   other side,
> But behold! It has room enough—in it, hundreds and
>   thousands,—all the varieties.[3]

Whitman's appreciation of art dated at least from his *Eagle* days and intensified greatly in the early fifties, when he hobnobbed with Brooklyn daguerreotypists and artists. A third of his thirty-seven articles published between 1849 and 1855 commented on art, and five were devoted solely to it. So involved in the art scene did he become that he was invited to address the opening meeting of the Brooklyn Art Union in 1851 and was subsequently nominated for the presidency of the Union.

Photography's ability to reflect reality would always remain for Whitman its chief attraction. He once declared: "The photograph has this advantage: it lets nature have its way: the botheration with the painters is that they don't want nature to have its way."[4] The more realistic moments in his poetry owed much to the vogue of the daguerreotype in America. Introduced in New York in 1839, the daguerreotype achieved a popularity in America unmatched abroad, where legal restraints interfered with its commercialization. By 1853 there were more daguerreotype studios in Manhattan alone than in all of England, and more on Broadway than in

London. By then, around three million daguerreotypes were produced annually in the United States.

Whitman registered photography's place in modern culture in his poems. In one he mentions "The implements for daguerreotyping," and in another he writes, "The camera and plate are prepared, the lady must sit for her daguerreotype."[5] Even more important than such explicit references were ideas about popular art he absorbed from the daguerreotype scene. Among those responsible for America's distinction in the new art form were three daguerreotypists he knew and admired: John Plumbe, Jr., Mathew B. Brady, and Gabriel Harrison. All three were prize-winning daguerreotypists who ran the popular galleries he frequented.

Whitman got through the Welsh-born Plumbe one of his earliest exposures to the exhibition-gallery experience. After touring Plumbe's gallery in July 1846 he wrote: "You will see more *life* there, more variety, more human nature, more artistic beauty (for what can surpass that masterpiece of human perfection, the human face?) than in any spot we know of." Whitman felt he was in the presence of "an immense phantom concourse—speechless and motionless, but yet *realities*," and he added: "Time, space, both are annihilated, and we identify the semblances with the reality."[6]

Photography seemed to provide a miraculous suspension of time and space by preserving the essence of individuals. This preservation of people's essential selves through pictures was a topic of conversation between Whitman and the era's leading photographer, Mathew Brady. Whitman often went to Brady's Broadway daguerreotype gallery and in 1846 called him "a capital artist" whose "pictures possess a peculiar life-likeness."[7] Whitman told Brady that he believed history could be best preserved through realistic portraits. Whitman's compulsion in *Leaves of Grass* to have everything "literally photographed" reflects his faith in the power of photography to absorb experience and hold it fast. In this sense, his poetic "I" was a kind of roving camera eye aimed at the world around him.

As the experiences of both Brady and Whitman would show, however, pictures do not reflect history in a straightforward way. Rather, they show the shaping hand of the photographer, who can include or exclude people or things according to a particular vision of the world. Brady's most famous achievement in the 1840s and early '50s was the photographing of celebrities of all kinds, particularly political leaders. When people of different viewpoints— often political enemies—were grouped together in daguerreotype dignity as "illustrious Americans," a kind of visual utopia was created in which sectional hostilities and bitter personal rivalries were temporarily suspended. Brady's *Gallery of Illustrious Americans* (1850), published the year of the Compromise of 1850 (including the Fugitive Slave Act), showed the utopian possibilities of the daguerreotype. Juxtaposed in the volume were pictures of the Southern loyalist John C. Calhoun, the Northern antislavery editor Horace Greeley, the senatorial compromisers Henry Clay and Daniel Webster, and others, all conjoined in pictorial stateliness.

Like Brady, Whitman would perform a political balancing act in *Leaves of Grass*, in which proslavery types and their antislavery foes were "photographed" and put on exhibition. Whitman's "illustrious Americans," however, had little to do with the social leaders Brady had valorized. Between 1850 and '54 incompetence and corruption in high places eroded public confidence in the powers that be. Whitman, like the emerging Republican Party, fiercely rejected entrenched authority and advanced a new kind of popu-lism. As the Republicans would come up with the hardy western explorer John Frémont as their 1856 Presidential candidate, so Whitman advertised himself as "one of the roughs," an image pow-erfully communicated in the frontispiece portrait of the casually dressed Whitman in the 1855 edition of *Leaves of Grass*.

Whitman had known the artist behind the picture, the dag-guerotypist Gabriel Harrison, since the 1840s. Harrison was a pio-neer of the so-called "occupational" daguerreotype—that is, the picture of average, working-class people. When Harrison opened his studio on Fulton Street in Brooklyn, Whitman in the *Star* hailed Harrison as "one of the best Daguerrean operators probably in the world" and his pictures as "perfect works of truth and art."[8]

On a sweltering summer day in 1854 when Garrison saw Whitman on Fulton Street coming home from his carpenter job, he summoned him into his studio probably with the aim of pro-ducing an occupational daguerreotype. What he produced, as it turned out, combined the egalitarianism of the occupational with the resonance of the allegorical—an ideal combination for the poet who in 1855 wished to present himself as both the ordinary Ameri-can and the messianic Answerer.

In the picture Whitman stands with an air of I-am-your-equal, with his open shirt, rumpled pants, tilted hat, and grizzled face radiating egalitarianism. At the same time, there are unexpected depths and subtleties. The right hand is perched openly on the hip, but the left disappears into the pants, suggesting the bodily mysteries Whitman will be exploring. The expression of the face is full of emotional shadings: insolence, calmness, compassion, even a touch of sadness.

Whitman in 1854; from daguerreotype by Gabriel Harrison, copied by Samuel Hollyer onto a lithographic plate and reprinted opposite title plate of the 1855 *Leaves of Grass*.
Library of Congress, Prints and Photographs Division

Whitman's portrait showed an illustrious American for the mid-fifties: individualistic, defiant, rooted in the working-class consciousness that seemed to offer redemption in a time of failed social rulers. It pointed to the gallery of "photographs" in the early poetry—vignettes of common life promoting the artisanal values Whitman was holding up to the nation.

Photography offered an ideal of a direct mimesis of reality, supporting Whitman's oft-repeated aim of establishing an honest, personal relationship with the reader. He once told Traubel that the superiority of photographs to oils was that "they are honest."[9] He wrote in a poem, "The well-taken photographs—but your wife or friend close and solid in your arms?"[10] Here the photographic representation of the loved one is the catalyst for a fuller appreciation of the loved one's actual presence. The picture as a focusing of experience led back to life.

Antebellum painters had the same ethos as daguerreotypists: they strove for mimetic realism. Theirs, however, was a spiritualized realism, one that accorded at once with Whitman's earthly and religious sides. Accepting, like Whitman, the harmonious vision of the physical creation advanced by progressive scientists such as Humboldt and Agassiz, they pictured nature in detail but still retained a mystical aura that led in the fifties to the emergence of luminism. The pendulum swing in Whitman's poetry from earthly minutiae to mystical suggestion had precedent in a painting style that was at once mimetic and transcendental.

The art exhibits he frequented were filled with life-affirming, nature-affirming works: the Hudson River paintings of Thomas Cole, Asher B. Durand, and Thomas Doughty; the Greek revival sculpture of Horatio Greenough and Hiram Powers; the optimistic, intensely democratic genre paintings of William Sidney Mount and George Caleb Bingham; the peaceful luminist landscapes of Fitz Hugh Lane, Sanford Gifford, and John F. Kensett; the grand, epic luminist canvases of Frederic Edwin Church.

The American paintings of the period were democratic in style and subject matter. They minimized the painterly and stylized on behalf of the direct, the accessible, the transparent. In nature paintings, the main effort was to enable the average viewer to experience God's creation afresh, particularly in the form of still landscapes tinged with luminist iridescence. In genre paintings, the effort was enable ordinary folk to see slightly idealized versions of themselves in action, at work or play.

There were many practitioners of these principles between 1830 and 1860 in addition to several theorists, most notably the sculptor Horatio Greenough, who argued that ornament must be stripped away and artistic form should be natural rather than artificial. Anticipating Whitman, Greenough believed that America desperately needed art and artists. He called for a democratic art that was simple, unembellished. Along with naturalness came experimentation. He noted that in nature "there is no arbitrary law of proportion, no unbending model of form," and so artists should "*encourage experiment* at the risk of license, rather than submit to an iron rule." Greenough was also a chief figure in the American treatment of the nude. He wrote of "the human frame, the most beautiful organization of earth, the exponent and minister of the highest being we immediately know."[11]

Whitman's search for a transparent, democratic style free of artifice and close to nature's forms was akin to this artistic theory. In the 1855 preface he labeled "a nuisance and revolt" anything that "distorts honest shapes," specifying that in paintings or illustrations or sculptures Americans "shall receive no pleasure from violations of natural models and must not permit them."[12] Just as Greenough argued that art should follow nature's rhythms, so Whitman wrote, "The rhyme and uniformity of perfect poems show the free growth of metrical laws and bud from them as unerringly and loosely as lilacs or roses on a bush, and take shapes as compact as the shapes of chestnuts and oranges and melons and pears, and shed the perfume impalpable to form." Following the democratic trend to get directly back to the creation in art, Whitman gave the Adamic promise of unadulterated, sun-washed nature and a return to origins:

> Stop this day and night with me and you shall possess the
>   origin of all poems,

You shall possess the good of the earth and sun (there are
   millions of suns left,)
You shall no longer take things at second or third hand.[13]

At times, he could borrow directly from specific paintings. The
artistic school he usually tapped was genre painting. For subject
matter, the American genre painters looked to hearty outdoor
types—farmers, hunters, trappers, riverboatmen. More often than
not, these subjects were portrayed good-humoredly engaged in
some form of leisurely, often prankish activity. Also, genre painting was one of the few public arenas in which Indians and blacks
were treated with less of the overt racism that permeated nearly
every aspect of American society.

Whitman's relationship with two artists who treated Native
Americans—George Catlin and Alfred Jacob Miller—are particularly telling. Catlin, the foremost antebellum artist of the American West and the Indians, struck Whitman as a strongly American
artist whose works were national treasures. Whitman got to know
Catlin, who before going to Europe gave him a painting of the
Seminole chief Osceola, which became the basis of Whitman's
poem "Osceola," depicting the tragedy of that heroic Native
American who died as result of treachery by whites.

The humanization of minorities in American art had a strong
influence on Whitman. The section of "Song of Myself" picturing the marriage of the trapper and the Indian woman was based
on *The Trapper's Bride*, an often-reproduced painting by the Baltimore artist Alfred Jacob Miller. Miller showed how the tabooed
topic of miscegenation could be handled frankly and without apol-
ogy. In Miller's rendering of the theme, the trapper stands with
his bride as friends and family watch nearby. Whitman gives an

almost identical picture: an Indian tribe watches as a bearded trapper, dressed in buckskin, leans on his rifle as he grasps the hand of his bride, whose long hair frames her body.[14] Miller's painting had opened up possibilities for racial harmony and love, and Whitman followed suit.

Another of Whitman's scenes of racial harmony, the later passage in "Song of Myself" about the African American team driver, also had precedent in genre paintings, particularly those of the Long Island artist William Sidney Mount. The influential Mount, whose works crowded the New York galleries, became famous in part because of his paintings of blacks. Whitman in an article mentioned having seen "Mount's last work—I think his best—of a Long Island negro, the winner of a goose at raffle."[15] It is likely Whitman and Mount knew each other.

Particularly suggestive among Mount's paintings in terms of Whitman's portrayal of blacks is *Farmer's Nooning* (1835). The painting shows five farmers—three white men, a white boy, and a large black man—resting by a tree and a haystack at noon hour. The black man is strategically foregrounded: He is the only adult lying in the sun rather than in the shade, and he is the only one whose full body and face are shown. He is a massive, handsome man clad in a sparkling white, open shirt and tan pants. As he lies on the ground, his arms outspread, a young white boy is playfully tickling his face with a piece of straw. The theme of racial intermingling and comradeship is underscored by Mount's positioning of the figures. All the bodies blend into each other because they overlap on the canvas. Mount creates a picturesque moment of racial harmony.

Whitman evokes a similar spirit in his passage about the black team driver:

The negro holds firmly the reins of his four horses, the block
     swags underneath on its tied-over chain,
The negro that drives the huge dray of the stone-yard, steady
     and tall he stands pois'd on one leg on the string-piece, [...]
His glance is calm and commanding, he tosses the slouch of his
     hat away from his forehead,
The sun falls on his crispy hair and moustache, falls on the
     black of his polish'd and perfect limbs.

I behold the picturesque giant and love him, and I do not stop
     there,
I go with the team also.[16]

The pictorial quality of this racially bonding passage is unmis-
takable. Whitman calls the driver "the picturesque giant" and
emphasizes his aesthetic, ennobling features. Even more than
Mount's massive black, Whitman's is foregrounded, since he is
not framed by whites but stands tall and commanding in his
driver's seat. As in Mount, his open shirt exposes his upper chest
and the sun suffuses his black body, highlighting its beauty and
brawn. The gesture toward racial harmony made in Mount's poem
is repeated in Whitman's passage, which ends with the "I" sitting
by the black man as he drives his team.

Whitman and Mount shared an interest in the homey details of
everyday life and people, usually with an emphasis on the joyful
activity of country or artisan types. Just as Mount liked to capture
workers in moments of recreation or ease (e.g., rural folk dancing
or playing instruments or just idling), so Whitman chants of lazily
contemplating the grass or of common workers singing songs.
Just as Mount represents the activity and movement of common
life, so Whitman captures varied subjects in the midst of everyday

activities, relying heavily on active verbs or participles. When Whitman's friend John Burroughs described the poet's catalogs as "one line genre word paintings," he doubtless had in mind the kind of crisp, lively vignettes Mount had popularized in such paintings as *Bargaining for a Horse*, *Eel Spearing at Setauket*, and *Ringing the Pig*.[17]

As with Mount, even the most common activities take on interest for Whitman. It is not far from Mount's artistic sensibility to that of Whitman, who generated catalogs like this:

> The one-year wife is recovering and happy, having a week ago
> borne her first child,
> The clean-hair'd Yankee girl works with her sewing-machine or
> in the factory or mill,
> The pavingman leans on his two-handed rammer, the
> reporter's lead flies swiftly over the note-book, the sign-
> painter is lettering with blue and gold,
> The canal boy trots on the tow-path, the book-keeper counts at
> his desk, the shoemaker waxes his thread.[18]

Elsewhere in this catalog Whitman writes, "The connoisseur peers along the exhibition-gallery with half-shut eyes bent sideways." Whitman's catalogs as a whole are a kind of exhibition-gallery, reflecting the democratic eclecticism in the antebellum galleries where Mount and others exhibited. Mount was hardly alone among artistic precursors of Whitman's catalogs. The Missouri painter George Caleb Bingham, a Western version of Mount, produced popular genre studies of frontier types that Whitman knew of. Bingham's *The Jolly Boatman* (1846), notable for its vernacular treatment of frolicking flatboatmen, may have influenced vignettes in Whitman's poetry, such as this one: "Flatboatmen make fast towards dusk near the cotton-wood or pecan-trees, / Coon-seekers go through the regions of the Red river or through those drain'd by the Tennessee, or through those of the Arkansas." There is also a similarity between Bingham's painting *Shooting for the Beef* (1850) and Whitman's account of a Western turkey-shoot.

While genre painting contributed to the catalogs, in a larger sense Whitman was committed to the union of matter and spirit, the real and the ideal that informed antebellum painting as a whole. He responded favorably to two leaders of the Hudson River school, Thomas Doughty, whom he called "the prince of landscapists" and "the best of American painters," and Asher Durand, about whom he wrote, "all he does is good."[19] These painters modified the ideal, allegorical style of their fellow-Hudson River artist Thomas Cole, turning to a near-photographic style in the faith that nature in its unembellished details always pointed toward God's harmonious universe.

Whitman joined his contemporaries by picturing light and its prismatic refractions. The light that floods luminist painting, suggesting God's immanence and man's goodness, is akin to the light that plays through his poetry. A particular analogy can be made between him and Fredric Edwin Church, who forged an epic luminism by depicting vast, light-filled landscapes on huge canvases. These landscapes affirmed both the grandeur of the physical world and the ever-present possibility for transcendence.

Whitman similarly registered the vast effects of light. "Give me the splendid silent sun with all his beams full-dazzling," he wrote. His poem "A Prairie Sunset" pictured an expansive landscape aglow with the full range of colors:

Shot gold, maroon and violet, dazzling silver, emerald, fawn,
The earth's whole amplitude and Nature's multiform power
    consign'd for once to colors;
The light, the general air possess'd by them—colors till now
    unknown,
No limit, confine—not the Western sky alone—the high
    meridian—North, South, all,
Pure, luminous colors fighting the silent shadows to the last.[20]

Like Church, Whitman here transforms a colorful landscape into a metaphor for cosmic unity. The colors are varied, but they have a unifying effect because they encompass the entire scene and, by association, the whole world.

The luminist tendency to see an idealizing light everywhere enabled him to update the traditional religious image of the halo. In his poem "To You" he recreated Christian art in modern, luminist fashion:

Painters have painted their swarming groups and the centre-
    figure of all,
From the head of the centre-figure spreading a nimbus of gold-
    color'd light,
But I paint myriads of heads, but paint no head without its
    nimbus of gold-color'd light,
From my hand the brain of every man and woman it streams,
    effulgently flowing forever.

This passage states directly an implied message of much ante-bellum art: the potential divinity of mankind. Whitman is as interested in the light emanating from humans as in the light that suffuses nature.

Despite real affinities between Whitman and contemporary painters, there were important differences. He knew the rough, turbulent aspects of American experience, and he saw that they were minimized by the main Hudson River painters. He wanted picturesqueness but also explosiveness, rebelliousness, suggestiveness.

Late in life he would discover these qualities in the French painter Jean-François Millet. He found in *The Sower* (1850), Millet's famous study of peasant life, "a sublime murkiness and original fury," reminding him of the explosive cultural forces behind the French Revolution.[21] In Millet's works Whitman felt "the untold something behind all that was depicted—an essence, a suggestion, an indirection, leading off into the immortal mysteries."[22] He felt such a kinship with Millet that he once said his poems were "really only Millet in another form—they are the Millet that Walt Whitman has succeeded in putting into words." There is no evidence, however, that he had been aware of Millet before he had produced the early editions of *Leaves of Grass.*

Although Whitman did not find a Millet on the antebellum scene, he made what use he could of the artistic materials America had to offer. He spent a lot of time in the Brooklyn studio of the sculptor Henry Kirke Brown, whose work he admired. He also befriended many other artists, including the young sculptor John Quincy Adams Ward, the landscapist and portrait painter Frederick A. Chapman, and the Hudson River landscapist Jesse Talbot.

There was one American artist Whitman thought showed especially great promise: the Brooklyn portrait painter Walter Libbey. He found in Libbey's work the texturing and suggestiveness that was absent from the prevailing hard-surfaced style. He especially praised a Libbey portrait of a casually dressed country boy playing a flute while seated on a river bank. "There is no hardness," Whitman wrote, "and the eye is not pained by the sharpness of outline which mars many otherwise fine pictures. In the scene of the background, and in all the accessories, there is a delicious melting in, so to speak, of object with object; an effect that is frequent enough in nature, though painters seem to disdain following it."[23] It was this "melting in" quality that Whitman missed in much American art and which he tried to attain in several artistic moments in his poetry. With all his attention to vivid particularities, he also strained toward vista and suggestiveness, as in this line: "A show of summer softness—a contact of something unseen—an amour of the light and air."[24]

Like most antebellum artists, however, Libbey failed to absorb the wild, agitated, radical idioms that represented the more subversive elements of American society and politics. Whitman took it upon himself to push American art theory toward a broad, inclusive realm that had room for the full range of experience, from the placidly beautiful to the rebellious and explosive.

His speech before the Brooklyn Art Union, delivered on March 31, 1851, promoted his idea that art was desperately needed by an increasingly materialistic society and extended the idea of art to include all heroic actions, especially revolutionary or subversive ones. He gave as examples of artistic action the self-sacrifice of "all great rebels and innovators," including the Hungarian revolutionary Kossuth, the exiled Italian rebel Mazzini, and others.[25] He concluded the address with a recitation of the lines from his own poem "Resurgemus" about the corpses of murdered young rebels nurturing the seeds of freedom and revolt against tyrants all over the earth.

This was Whitman trying to bring social and political conscience to American art, which by and large was politically complacent in his day. The fact that he ended his Art Union address with a passage from a political poem laced with the barbed rhetoric of working-class protest showed him trying to push American art in a new, radical direction.

His interest in the Art Union was part of his overriding desire to organize artists everywhere so that they might reform American society. If he hoped that groups like the Brooklyn Art Union would contribute to this social reorganization, he soon learned otherwise. Although he was nominated for the presidency of the Union in the spring of 1851, the group quickly fizzled.

But Whitman's faith in the socially transforming powers of art did not die. To the contrary, it was given fresh life by the opening in the summer of 1853 of the world art and industry exhibition at New York's Crystal Palace. This long event was the culminating moment of antebellum exhibition culture.

In Whitman's eyes, the Crystal Palace itself was a work of art. Covering nearly five acres in the area of what is now Bryant Park, near 42nd Street, the building was shaped like a tremendous Greek cross, with pane-glass ceilings and a towering dome at the intersection. Whitman called the Crystal Palace "an edifice certainly unsurpassed anywhere for beauty and all other requisites for a perfect edifice . . . an original, esthetic, perfectly proportioned American edifice—one of the few that put modern times not beneath old times, but on an equality with them."[26] He was equally taken with the multifaceted exhibit it housed. He was irresistibly attracted to it, recalling later, "*New York, Great Exposition open'd in 1853*. I went a long time (nearly a year)—days and nights—especially the latter."[27]

The Crystal Palace was antebellum America's grandest attempt to make art available to the general public. The authors of the exhibition catalog wrote that "the power of Art to educate and refine the masses" would be realized only "when its works are no longer a monopoly, but an every-day possession, within the reach of the mechanic and the tradesman as well as the opulent and noble."[28] The Crystal Palace promised to help fulfill Whitman's dream of transforming society through art, since, for the first time on a grand scale, the American masses could be exposed to art on a regular basis.

This was art in the most inclusive sense. On the one hand, there was a full range of paintings, daguerreotypes, and sculptures. Alongside such art works were displayed elaborate chinaware and tapestries, the cotton gin, the electric telegraph, a fire engine, different pistols, the Adams printing press, and other instruments. It was a potpourri of the modern and the neoclassical, the artistic and the mechanical that lent credence to Whitman's idea that art could be defined flexibly and broadly. He saw beauty and wonder in machines and liked to exhibit them in his poetry:

> The cylinder press . . . the handpress . . . the frisket and tympan
> . . . the compositor's stick and rule,
> The implements for daguerreotyping . . . the tools of the rigger
> or grappler or sailmaker or blockmaker, [. . .]
> The walkingbeam of the steam-engine . . . the throttle and
> governors, and the up and down rods.[29]

That his catalogs are linked to antebellum exhibition culture is made clear by the unfinished and uncollected pre-1855 poem "Pictures," which has survived in a faded notebook. The poem outdid even the heterogeneous exhibits in the Crystal Palace in the eclecticism of its images. Whitman had long sought an organizing principle to coordinate the wide range of people and things he viewed as artistic. He was discovering that organizing principle in his poetic "I."

He begins the poem with the startling image of his own head as a gallery with "many pictures hanging suspended" and repeats the motif at the end: "And every hour of the day and night has given me copious pictures." The picture gallery here is being internalized and identified with the poetic imagination. Whitman presents quick vignettes from history—Adam in Paradise, Christ, a Hindu sage, Socrates with his students, the Battle of Brooklyn—and even enters the spirit world, describing "Phantoms, countless, men and women, after death, wandering." Recent American history is included with pictures of Jefferson and Emerson. He uses the exhibition trope to personalize his yoking together of various geographical regions, as he speaks of "my" Southern slavegrounds, "my" Kansas life, "my" Oregon hut, and so on. He introduces an urban element absent from most antebellum art by celebrating "the young man of Mannahatta—the celebrated rough," adding emphatically: "The one I love so much—let others sing whom they may—him I sing for a thousand years!"[30]

Five

SCIENCE, PHILOSOPHY, AND RELIGION

"LO! KEEN-EYED TOWERING SCIENCE, / AS FROM TALL PEAKS THE MODERN overlooking," writes Whitman in "Song of the Universal." In the next breath he adds, "Yet again, lo! the soul, above all science."[1]

These lines point to the movement in his poetry from the scientific to the spiritual. He struggled to bring together the two in his poetry, and he made use of popular approaches that made such couplings possible.

Like the eighteenth-century deists, he denied the specialness of any single religion and forged a broadly ecumenical outlook that embraced all religions. As he wrote, his was "the greatest of faiths and the least of faiths." His ecumenical outlook engendered two long passages in "Song of Myself" in which he listed by name the major world religions, indicating that he respected and accepted them all. He surveyed them again in "With Antecedents" and affirmed: "I adopt each theory, myth, god, and demi-god, /

I see that the old accounts, bibles, genealogies, are true, without exception."

He accepted all religions but believed in no single church. It was difficult for him to have faith in the churches at a time when he felt they had become poisoned by association with economic injustice and chattel slavery. "The churches," he wrote Emerson in 1856, "are one vast lie; the people do not believe them, and they do not believe themselves. . . . The spectacle is a pitiful one." In the scathing poem "Respondez!" Whitman wrote: "Let churches accommodate serpents, vermin, and the corpses of those who have died of the most filthy of diseases! / [. . .]Let there be no God!"[2]

Often his doubts about the churches merged into skepticism about larger matters. He frequently meditated on death in his writings. "Not a day passes, not a minute or second without a corpse," he writes in one poem; "Slow-moving and black lines creep over the whole earth—they never cease—they are the burial lines."[3] His poetry is scattered with the dead: the 412 soldiers slaughtered at Goliad, the drowned swimmer, the mashed fireman, the lost she-bird, Lincoln, the Civil War dead.

Pondering death brought him to the brink of doubt. He knew, as he wrote in "Song of Myself," the feeling "That life is a suck and a sell, and nothing remains at the end but threadbare crepe and tears."[4] He could identify with bitter atheists:

Down-hearted doubters dull and excluded,
Frivolous, sullen, moping, angry, affected, dishearten'd,
    atheistical,
I know every one of you, I the sea of torment, doubt, despair,
    and unbelief.[5]

Whitman, however, had wide-ranging strategies for combating doubt. One he found in physical science. Among the scientists who offered hopeful explanations of nature was the Stockholm chemist Justus Liebig. When the American edition of Liebig's *Chemistry in Its Application to Physiology and Agriculture* appeared in 1847, Whitman raved about it in the *Eagle*. "Chemistry!" he wrote. "The elevating, beautiful, study ... which involves the essences of creation, and the changes, and the growths, and formations and decays of so large a constituent part of the earth, and the things thereof!" Liebig's fame was "as wide as the civilized world—a fame nobler than that of generals, or of many bright geniuses."[6]

Liebig presented a scientific rationale for what would become one of Whitman's main answers to cynics: even if matter were all, nature constantly regenerates itself and turns death into life through chemical transformation. Liebig gave the idea of the cycle of nature validity through the study of transferred chemical compounds. When people and animals died, their atoms became transferred to the earth and plant life, whose atoms in turn became the source of new life. Whatever diseases they had were lost in the transforming process.

There seemed, then, to be an ongoing resurrection and a democratic exchange of substances inherent in nature. Just as Liebig wrote that "the active state of the atoms of one body has an influence upon the atoms of a body in contact with it," so Whitman announced in the second line of his opening poem that "every atom belonging to me as good belongs to you."[7] As Liebig said that after death humans are changed into other things, so Whitman could write: "We are Nature [...] / We become plants, trunks, foliage, roots, bark, / We are bedded in the ground, we are rocks, /

We are oaks."[8] If Liebig envisaged an exchange of life forms through decomposition and regrowth, so Whitman fashioned metaphors that vivified the idea of the ceaseless springing of life from death: "Tenderly will I use you curling grass, / It may be you transpire from the breasts of young men"; "The smallest sprout shows there is really no death"; "And as to you Corpse I think you are good manure."[9] Liebig wrote that "the miasms and certain contagious matters [that] produce diseases in the human organism" become "not *contagious*" when the organism is absorbed into the earth.[10] This becomes the central point of Whitman's poem "This Compost." He asks the earth in amazement: "Are they not continually putting distemper'd corpses within you? / [...]Where have you drawn off all the foul and liquid meat?"[11] He provides the Liebigian answer:

What chemistry!
That the winds are really not infectious, [...]
That all is clean forever and forever.

Whitman also found in science confirmation of his optimistic instincts about the origin and nature of humans and their place in nature. Most scientists before Darwin were not pessimistic about nature and species. What might be called a "progressive consensus" emerged among naturalists and biologists. This outlook found expression in several immensely popular books, including the Edinburgh biologist Robert Chambers' *Vestiges of the Natural History of Creation* (1844) and the Prussian geographer Alexander von Humboldt's *Kosmos*, published in four volumes between 1845 and 1857. In 1846 the Swiss naturalist Louis Agassiz relocated to the United States, devoting the remaining decades of his life to promoting an idealistic version of progressive science.

According to the progressive view, the universe was formed of gases that developed constantly toward man. (By a poetic metonymy, Whitman enacted this idea when he wrote in "Crossing Brooklyn Ferry," "I too had been struck from the float forever held in solution").[12] The earth was not young, as the Bible suggested and as previous scientists had believed, but instead was very old; the Scottish geologist James Hutton actually called it indefinitely old. Although the earth's extreme age seemed to contravene the Bible's teachings, the scientists in general did not abandon religious faith.

To the contrary, they believed that every aspect of physical creation revealed a divine plan. They accepted the so-called argument from design, introduced in the late seventeenth century and given fresh life by William Paley's classic *Natural Theology* (1802), which taught that everything in the universe was so well adapted to its uses that it revealed God's benignity. The elegantly efficient joints of the hand and the intricate mechanism of the eye were the kinds of everyday miracles the scientists pointed to. When the Harpers brought out a new edition of *Natural Theology* in 1847, Whitman argued that it gave scientific proof of the sacredness of physical things.

In Whitman's poems, the optimism of progressive science is figured forth as heady exuberance. No scientific idealist reveled in common natural experience to the extent he did. The "I" of "Song of Myself" announces that his armpit aroma is finer than any prayer, that his head is finer than all the churches and creeds, that a mouse is miracle enough to stagger sextillions of infidels. In another poem Whitman writes, "How beautiful and perfect are the animals! / How perfect the earth, and the minutest thing upon it!"[13] All of these images argue from design with a vengeance. If the scientists called the earth indefinitely old, Whitman exulted in the sense of infinity: "A few quadrillions of eras, a few octillions of cubic leagues, [...] / They are but parts ... any thing is but a part."[14] Just as several scientists believed that people have evolved upward through many different organisms, he called life "the leavings of many deaths" and added, "No doubt I have died myself ten thousand times before." He poeticizes the pre-Darwinian evolutionary theory, complete with nebula and progress over time through varied forms:

Before I was born out of my mother generations guided me,
My embryo has never been torpid, nothing could overlay it.

For it the nebula cohered to an orb, [...]
Monstrous sauroids transported it in their mouths and
    deposited it with care.

All forces have been steadily employ'd to complete and delight me,
Now on this spot I stand with my robust soul.

To communicate his sense of embodying all time and nature, Whitman fastened on the word "kosmos." The word was so important to him that it was the only one he retained in the different versions of his famous self-identification in "Song of Myself," which first read, "Walt Whitman, an American, one of the roughs, a kosmos," and ended up as, "Walt Whitman, a kosmos, of Manhattan the son." The word had been popularized by Alexander von Humboldt, whose multivolume *Kosmos* was well received and immediately translated into several languages; the English title was *Cosmos: A Sketch of a Physical Description of the Universe.*

Humboldt pictured nature not in chaos or conflict but as a source of calmness, always in equilibrium, with humans as the acme of creation. "Cosmos" signified both the order of nature and the centrality of human beings. "Cosmos" was ready-made for poetic adaptation, since it gathered together nature, intuition, and art. Whitman in his poem "Kosmos" (he retained the "k" of the German) associated the word with a person in tune with all things, one

> Who includes diversity and is Nature,
> Who is the amplitude of the earth, and the coarseness and
>   sexuality of the earth, and the great charity of the earth, and
>   the equilibrium also, [...]
> Who, constructing the house of himself or herself, not for a day
>   but for all times, sees races, eras, dates, generations,
> The past, the future, dwelling there, like space, inseparable
>   together.

The circle of scientists and pseudoscientists surrounding Whitman, most of them associated with his early distributor Fowlers & Wells, had a special role in popularizing and Americanizing such progressive, optimistic ideas. Phrenology, the pseudoscience that taught that all character traits were produced by specific brain organs, became in the hands of his friends Orson and Lorenzo Fowler a system of self-help for all aspects of the human being, physical and spiritual.

After hearing Orson Fowler lecture in 1846, Whitman rejoiced over the phrenological idea that any mental faculty could be developed through exercise. Whitman wrote, "If the professor can, as he professes, teach men to know their intellectual and moral deficiencies and remedy them, we do not see that our people may long remain imperfect."[15] On July 16, 1849, Whitman went to Clinton Hall to have his head examined by the quiet, learned

Lorenzo Fowler. He was doing nothing unusual. Among others who had their skulls read were Edgar Allan Poe, Margaret Fuller, Lydia Maria Child, and Mark Twain.

Whitman had reason to be pleased with the result of his skull exam. On a numbering system of one to seven (with the high score of seven indicating the largest size of a brain organ), Whitman got a six to seven in Self-Esteem and Caution and a six in Amativeness, Adhesiveness, Philoprogentiveness, Concentrativeness, and Combativeness. He must have been cheered by Fowlers' assessment, "You are yourself at all times," and puzzled by his low scores of four in Tune and five in Language—not good signs for a budding bard.[16] But Whitman was sufficiently happy that he published his phrenological chart on four different occasions. His interest in phrenology lasted long after the craze had died out. In old age he confessed, "I probably have not got by the phrenology stage yet."[17]

He also used phrenological terms throughout his poetry. In the 1855 preface he included the phrenologist among "the lawgivers of poets" and added phrenological force to his description of the poet by saying he has "large hope and comparison and fondness for women and children, large alimentiveness and destructiveness and causality."[18] Phrenology taught that everyone possessed a unique blend of characteristics, an idea communicated in the first version of "Song of the Broad-Axe":

> Never offering others always offering himself, corroborating his
>   phrenology,
> Voluptuous, inhabitive, combative, conscientious, alimentive,
>   intuitive, of copious friendship, sublimity, firmness, self-
>   esteem, comparison, locality, individuality, form, eventuality.[19]

The Fowlers had changed phrenology, mainly an intellectual concern abroad, into a popular program for self-help. The numbers they assigned to the various brain organs had a purpose: a low number suggested that a certain organ was too small and must be developed by exercise of that particular trait; a large number, by the same token, suggested that a trait had to be controlled so that it did not become dominant.

Above all, the Fowlers advised keeping the various brain organs and other bodily functions in equilibrium. Anything that threatened that balance could cause insanity or physical disease. It was not the brain alone that signaled well-being: All other bodily parts did too. Everything about a person—the walk, the laugh, the lips, eyes, skin, voice, gestures—betrayed character. Whitman echoed this holistic view in several poems, including "I Sing the Body Electric":

> [T]he expression of a well-made man appears not only in his
>   face,
> It is in his limbs and joints also, it is curiously in the joints of
>   his hips and wrists,
> It is in his walk, the carriage of his neck, the flex of his waist
>   and knees.[20]

What was most hopeful about the Fowlers' program was that they offered methods of repairing mental imbalances. One was vigorous self-reprimand. A person on the verge of addiction to a certain vice or excess was enjoined to shout inwardly against that vice. In outlining a remedy for the widespread vice of masturbation, for instance, Orson Fowler used capitalization to suggest how one should talk to oneself:

TOTAL ABSTINENCE IS LIFE; animal, intellectual, moral. INDULGENCE IS TRIPLE DEATH! RESOLUTION . . . STOP NOW AND FOREVER, or abandon all hope.[21]

Some of Whitman's most revealing notebook entries show that he had learned the technique of self-reprimand. In one entry he announced: "I have resolv'd to inaugurate for myself a pure per- fect sweet, cleanblooded robust body by ignoring all drinks but water and pure milk—and all fat meats later suppers—a great body— a purged, cleansed, spiritualised and invigorated body—."[22] This was straightforward Fowlerian self-control.

The most famous of all his notebook entries, the 1870 one in which he struggled to come to terms with his feelings toward his friend Peter Doyle, showed him again using the kind of self- reprimand the Fowlers had advised. Phrenologists regarded ad- hesiveness, or friendship between people of the same sex, as an essential part of the human mind. But when either adhesiveness or amativeness (heterosexual love) became overactive, the results on the mind could be disastrous. As Orson Fowler wrote, "When inflamed, fevered, dissatisfied, or irritated, [the social organs] in- flame every other portion of the brain, throwing it into violent commotion, especially the *animal propensities*; but if their action is natural, if they are properly placed, they put to rest the other animal propensities."[23]

When struggling with his feelings about Doyle in his diary, Whitman wrestled with such inflamed feelings. He warned himself

TO GIVE UP ABSOLUTELY *& for good, from the present hour, this* FEVERISH, FLUCTUATING, *useless*, UNDIGNIFIED PURSUIT *of 16.4* [Peter Doyle]—*too long, (much too long)*

persevered in,—so humiliating— —*It must come at last & had better come now—(It cannot possibly be a success)* LET THERE FROM THIS HOUR BE NO FALTERING, NO GETTING *at all henceforth* (NOT ONCE, *under any circumstances*) *—avoid seeing her* [originally "him"], *or meeting her, or any talk or explanations —or* ANY MEETING WHATEVER, FROM THIS HOUR FORTH, FOR LIFE July 15 '70

Outline sketch of a superb calm character [. . .]

Depress the adhesive nature /
It is in excess—making life a torment /
Ah this diseased, feverish, disproportionate adhesiveness /[24]

The most genuinely confessional of all Whitman's writings, this passage has been variously interpreted as an unequivocal expression of homosexuality and as a massive repression of the homosexual urge. But the vocabulary of modern psychology was not available to Whitman. He used instead phrenological self-regulation. Internalizing the language of the phrenologists, he says here that his "adhesiveness" has become "diseased, feverish, disproportionate" and warns himself to "Depress the adhesive nature." He is trying to bring this inflamed inclination under control, to regain mental equilibrium. His first strategy, as with the Fowlers, is self-reprimand. Just as they said that the first step toward self-correction was the "DETERMINATION TO STOP NOW AND FOREVER," so he tells himself "TO GIVE UP ABSOLUTELY" the pursuit of Doyle, warning sternly, "LET THERE FROM THIS HOUR BE NO FALTERING."

Interwoven with these strong resolutions are reminders of what a person in equilibrium is like. Whitman plans a sketch of "a superb calm character," echoing an earlier notebook entry in which he told himself to develop "A Cool, gentle (LESS DEMONSTRA-TIVE) MORE UNIFORM DEMEANOR" and "to live *a more Serene, Calm, Philosophic Life.—reticent, far more reticent*—yet cheerful, with pleased spirit and pleased manner."[25] Behind these reminders lay the phrenological conviction that inner balance could be gained through exercise of the will.

"Hurrah for positive science!" Whitman writes in "Song of Myself." "Long live exact demonstration!"; but then he says to scientists: "Your facts are useful, yet they are not my dwelling, / I but enter by them to an area of my dwelling."[26]

Religion and philosophy helped address some of the larger questions left unanswered by science. He generalized that from the start in his poetry "one deep purpose underlay the others, and has underlain it and its execution ever since—and that has been the religious purpose." The poet, in his words, was the "divine literatus" who replaced the priest.[27] America, he constantly stressed, could be rescued from materialism and infidelity only by literature that pointed to the spiritual and moral. He clung to a faith in immortality. "I am not prepared," he told Traubel, "to admit fraud in the scheme of the universe—yet without immortality all would be sham and sport of the most tragic nature."[28] His close Brooklyn friend Helen Price found his "leading characteristic" to be "the *religious sentiment* or feeling. It pervades and dominates his life."[29]

Whitman did not have much first-hand exposure to European Romantic philosophy but received it through edited collections like Frederick Henry Hedge's *Prose Writers of Germany*, which the poet called "a big valuable book."[30] All the philosophers in the volume accepted the argument from design that was an underpinning of progressive science. Sometimes their expression of the outlook approached a kind of pre-Whitmanian mysticism. The physiologist Johann Caspar Lavater emphasized the miraculous nature of apparently insignificant things: "Each particle of matter is an immensity; each leaf a world; each insect an inexplicable compendium."[31] Whitman would write in the same vein that a tree toad is the chef d'oeuvre of the highest, a leaf of grass is the journeywork of the stars, and so on.

Whitman observed American Protestantism with interest. The evangelical groups that grew most dramatically, especially the Methodists and Baptists, were promoted by an intense zeal manifested in conversion "exercises" like running, barking, dancing, convulsions, a zeal captured in Whitman's line about a religious convert "Ranting and frothing in my insane crisis."[32] Evangelical religion was spread by a vigorous, lively brand of preaching that made use of slang and humor. Brooklyn's Henry Ward Beecher made extensive use of jokes and illustrations. Whitman was rapturous about Beecher's pulpit style. In time, his fascination with popular preaching made him susceptible to the eloquence of the homespun sailors' preacher Edward Thompson Taylor, whom he called America's "one essentially perfect orator," and later to Brooklyn's T. DeWitt Talmage, whose lively sermons he enjoyed.

In a time when mainstream religion was becoming increasingly secular, promoters of religion could be thoroughly enjoyed without reference to the churches with which they were associated. Whitman wrote in his pre-1855 notebook, "The new theologies bring forward man."[33] Whitman separated someone like Beecher from church religion. "It was only fair to say of Beecher that he was not a minister," he said. "There was so much of him man there was little left of him to be minister."[34]

Not only did Whitman participate in the revolution in popular religious style, but *Leaves of Grass* in turn fed back into popular religion. Some of Whitman's images—such as the line in "Song of Myself," "I find letters from God dropt in the street, and every one is sign'd by God's name"—were picked up by Henry Ward Beecher, who found them thoroughly compatible with his folksy style.[35] Whitman called Beecher "a great absorber of Leaves of Grass" and he said he often met people who, having just heard Beecher preach, told him that "his whole sermon was you, you, you, from top to toe."[36]   Whitman was in tune not only with the stylistic revolution but with other dramatic changes in American religion. Surging revivalism, the throes of the market economy, and the rise of mass print culture combined to make nineteenth-century America a remarkably fertile breeding ground of new religions. The Shakers, the Mormons, the Oneidan perfectionists, Phoebe Palmer's perfectionist Methodists, the Seventh Day Adventists, the spiritualists, and the Harmonialists all sprang up between the Revolution and the Civil War. Several of the new movements were based on freshly inspired sacred writings meant to supplant or complement the Bible, such as William Smith's *The Book of Mormon* (1830) or Andrew Jackson Davis' *The Great Harmonia* (1850).

If other Americans were founding new religions, so, in a sense, was he: a poetic religion based on progressive science and idealist philosophy that preached the miracle of the commonplace and the possibilities of the soul. In promoting religion in his poetry, he could sound much like a nineteenth-century showman peddling wares: "Magnifying and applying come I, / Outbidding at the start the old cautious hucksters," as he went on to review all the world religions and then proclaim the miraculous nature of the everyday world.[37] He was conscious from the start about writing a supposedly inspired text. His messianic mission was made clear in the 1855 preface, in which he said of the poet, "The time straying toward infidelity and confections he withholds by his steady faith." He gave a recipe for salvation, including the command, "read these leaves in the open air every season of every year of your life." This mission became stronger with time, as evidenced by his June 1857 notebook entry: "*The Great Construction of the New Bible* / Not to be diverted from the principal object—the main life work—."[38] He saw that he was one of many who were initiating new religions:

> I too, following many and follow'd by many, inaugurate a
>   religion, I descend into the arena, [...]
> I say the real and permanent grandeur of these States must be
>   their religion,
> Otherwise there is no real and permanent grandeur.[39]

To place him in the camp of nineteenth-century Americans who were inaugurating new religions is not to say that he was solely preoccupied with American religious developments. His notebooks of the late 1850s betray a real interest in foreign and historical religions as well. The religion of ancient Egypt represented for him the miracle of life, as in its worship of the beetle and the sun. India to him meant rhapsody, passiveness, meditation, and Greece the celebration of beauty and the natural world. Christianity stood for love, gentleness, morality, and purity, although he noted its history of harsh penances and religious wars.

The fact remains, however, that if he had much exposure to foreign religions before 1855, he apparently left few records of it. For example, when Thoreau asked him in 1856 whether he had

Whitman in the late 1850s. *Ed Folsom Collection*

read the Asian scriptures, he replied, "No: tell me about them."[40] Surveying the poetry of the first two editions of *Leaves of Grass*, we find many things that appear to echo foreign religion or philosophy but could just as easily have sprung from one or more of several interrelated popular movements that crested in the 1850s: mesmerism, spiritualism, Swedenborgianism, and Harmonialism.

Mesmerism, which began as hypnotic mind-control and developed into a system of healing, popularized the terminology of animal magnetism that lay behind Whitman's images of electricity and fluid energy. Mesmerists argued that all phenomena were linked by a magnetic, electrical ether or fluid, called the odic force. Certain people, called "operators," had the ability to use their odic powers to magnetize, or place in a trance, other people, who thus became "subjects" or "mediums." Whitman wrote that "the science of animal magnetism...reveals at once the existence of whole new world of truth, grand, fearful, profound, relating to that great mystery, in the shadow of which we live and move and have our being."[41]

Whitman's use of the vocabulary of animal magnetism and electricity shows the mesmerists' influence. John Bovee Dods, a leading mesmerist, wrote, "Electricity, as a universal agent, pervades the entire atmosphere," governing all the operations of nature and linking nature to God.[42] So well attuned to the electrical theory was Whitman that at times his poetic persona seems like a bundle of electrical impulses. "I have instant conductors all over me whether I pass or stop," he writes in "Song of Myself," "They seize every object and lead it harmlessly through me."[43] His praise of the body and sex took on a cleansing, mystical quality when expressed in electrical language:

I sing the body electric,

The armies of those I love engirth me and I engirth them,

They will not let go of me till I go with them, respond to them,

And discorrupt them, and charge them full with the charge of
    the soul.

Allied to mesmerism was spiritualism, which also influenced Whitman. In its popular form, spiritualism emerged in 1848 in upstate New York when two impressionable teenaged girls heard strange knocking sounds that they claimed were produced by a spirit. The case set off a craze for spiritualist séances, in which "mediums" communicated with the dead. The presence of spirits was indicated by rapping, chair-moving, table-lifting, flying objects, and so on. A number of famous mediums, notably Cora Hatch and Anna Henderson, gave well attended lectures on the afterlife while in a trance state. In the 1850s, trance writing and trance lecturing was performed by hundreds who claimed to have spiritual gifts. Several volumes of trance poetry were published.

Whitman watched the spiritualist movement with genuine curiosity. He noted that the movement was "spreading with great rapidity." He estimated nearly five million American adherents of spiritualism and wrote: "There can be no doubt, that the spiritual movement is blending itself in many ways with society, in theology, in the art of healing, in literature, and in the moral and mental character of the people of the United States."[44]

One of the things it blended with was his poetry. In the 1855 preface he includes the "spiritualist" among "the lawgivers of poets."[45] His repeated assurances about immortality retain the optimism of the spiritualists. With the confidence of the spiritualist he announces, "I know I am deathless, […] I laugh at what you call dissolution."[46] In a self-review of the 1855 edition, he said of himself: "He is the true spiritualist. He recognizes no annihilation, or death, or loss of identity."[47]

On some level, the poet became associated in his mind with the spiritualist medium. As he wrote in his notebook, "The poets are divine mediums—through them come spirits and materials to all the people, men and women."[48] In a poem titled "Mediums" he says that a new race of mediums is arising that will "convey gospels" about nature, physiology, oratory, and death.[49] He used the vocabulary of spiritualism in other poems: "O! mediums! O to teach! to convey the invisible faith!," and, "Something unproved! something in a trance!"[50] In a "Calamus" poem he feels surrounded by "the spirits of dear friends dead or alive, thicker they come." Another poem describes "the rapt promises and luminè of seers, the spiritual world."[51]

Closely associated in his mind with spiritualism was Swedenborgianism. In an 1857 article he identified Emanuel Swedenborg as "the Spiritualist" and insisted that "his spiritual discoveries have special reference to America."[52] Swedenborg's doctrine of "correspondences" held that every material thing had a spiritual counterpart, or "ultimate." His was a body-specific, erotic mysticism. He described God as the Divine Man, who speaks to humans through the head or heart by "influx," or "divine breath."

Whitman averred that Swedenborg would have "the deepest and broadest mark upon the religions of future ages here, of any man that ever walked the earth." Like Emerson and Henry James, Sr., he found appealing Swedenborg's doctrine of correspondences. The Swedenborgian idea that everything has a spiritual essence is echoed in his lines in "Starting from Paumanok":

[H]aving look'd at the objects of the universe, I find there is no
one nor any particle of one but has reference to the soul.
Was somebody asking to see the soul?
See, your own shape, countenance, persons, substances, beasts,
the trees, the running rivers, the rocks and sands.[53]

"Crossing Brooklyn Ferry" makes use of a similar idea, as the
city and the commercial river traffic are called "dumb, beautiful
ministers" of which "none else is perhaps more spiritual," and all
"furnish your parts toward the soul."[54] His longest and most fervent poem in this vein was "Eidólons," the title of which was his
word for the Swedenborgian "ultimate." The poet looks everywhere and sees only the spiritual counterpart of every physical
and emotional thing.

Swedenborg's mysticism was inherently body-specific, as believers were thought to communicate with God through particular parts of the body. The lungs were said to play a key role in
spiritual communion. The "divine breath," also called the "influx" or "afflatus," was taken in from the spiritual atmosphere
through the lungs, which in turn emanated an "efflux" of its own
into the atmosphere. The Swedenborgian terms "influx," "efflux,"
and "afflatus" are used in the early editions of *Leaves of Grass*.
The "I" of "Song of Myself" calls himself the "Partaker of influx
and efflux" and declares: "Through me the afflatus surging and
surging . . . through me the current and index." In "Song of the
Open Road" Whitman writes: "Here is the efflux of the soul, / The
efflux of the soul comes from within through embower'd gates,
ever provoking questions."[55] Like the post-Swedenborgians of the
fifties, he could combine the notion of efflux with the "charge"
and universal fluid of animal magnetism:

The efflux of the soul is happiness, here is happiness,
I think it pervades the open air, waiting at all times,
Now it flows unto us, we are rightly charged.

Here rises the fluid and attaching character.

Swedenborg suggested to Whitman how the erotic and the mystical were linked. He told Traubel, "I think Swedenborg was right when he said there was a close connection—a very close connection—between the state we call religious ecstasy and the desire to copulate. I find it confirmed in all my experience."[56] Since the body was deeply involved in worship for the post-Swedenborgians, they often came up with physical metaphors for prayer. The soul for the Swedenborgians was no rarefied essence but almost a palpable other self.

This cultural background of erotic mysticism casts light on the section in "Song of Myself" in which the "I" describes lying with his soul on the grass on a transparent summer morning. The passage begins with a religious statement—"I believe in you my soul"—and leads through rapturous union to an affirmation of the peace and joy and love of God's universe.[57] The mixture of the physical and the spiritual is established at the start, when the persona says that neither the soul nor the body should be abased to each other. If Swedenborg could describe union with God as reception of the divine breath through the head or the chest, so Whitman could imagine the soul plunging its "tongue" into the "bare-stript heart" and spreading until it embraced the beard and feet. The expansive aftermath of the erotic-mystical union also has Swedenborgian overtones. In *Epic of the Starry Heavens* by the popular mystic Thomas Lake Harris (whom Whitman discussed in his notebooks) the soul, in its visionary flight to the divine world, encounters the spirits of countless men and women bound in love. Similarly, Whitman's "I" feels that he is bonded with all the men and women ever born and that a kelson of the creation is love.

His treatment of religious matters also had precedent in the Harmonial movement led by the famous "Poughkeepsie Seer," Andrew Jackson Davis, whom Whitman discussed at length with friends. While in a trance state, Davis could accomplish apparently miraculous things, such as reading books through walls and peering inside people's bodies to spot hidden diseases. In what he termed "traveling clairvoyance," Davis voyaged mentally to distant places and times.

Whitman participated in the trend of Harmonial mysticism. In a notebook entry of the period he wrote, "I am in a mystic trance exultation / Something wild and untamed—half savage."[58] In a later entry he described being "in a trance, yet with all senses alert" and with "the objective world suspended or surmounted for a while, & the powers in exaltation, freedom, vision."[59] The early editions of *Leaves of Grass* are filled with his versions of traveling clairvoyance. He outdid even Davis in his adventurous gamboling with time and space. In "Song of Myself" he writes: "My ties and ballasts leave me, I travel, my elbows rest in sea-gaps, / I skirt the sierras, my palms cover continents, / I am afoot with my vision."[60] If the trance writers mentally traversed history and space, so Whitman jumped rapidly between historical events (e.g., "Walking the old hills of Judea with the beautiful gentle God at my side") and distant places ("Speeding through space, speeding through heaven and the stars").

The spiritually healing powers of his persona bore the impress of the Harmonial outlook as expounded by Davis. The Harmonialists thought that electrical magnetism was perfectly in balance in nature and that by plunging into nature people could be physically healed and spiritually refreshed. The madly loving, sometimes sexual attraction to nature in the early editions of *Leaves of Grass* bore the Harmonial stamp. Whitman's persona embraces nature like a Harmonialist hungry for a magnetic charge:

> Press close bare-bosom'd night—press close magnetic
> nourishing night!
> Night of the south winds—night of the large few stars!
> Still nodding night—mad naked summer night.

Such "magnetic nourishing" power is supplied by virtually every facet of nature the "I" embraces. "Smile O voluptuous cool-breathed earth!" he proclaims. "Smile, for your lover comes." "You sea! I resign myself to you also [. . .] / Dash me with amorous wet, I can repay you." As with the Harmonialists, the sights, sounds, smells, touch of the physical world have magnetic reverberations in the poet's sensibility.

The sun had high significance for both the Harmonialists and Whitman. For the popular mystics, the sun was a chief source of the electrical fluid that permeated nature and quickened life. As the highest recipients of this magnetic energy, humans were thought to be extensions of the sun. In Thomas Lake Harris' poem, spirits in space congregate around suns and absorb odic force. Whitman's persona too is a "solar" man, responsive to the sun's special power and emanating an odic sun-force himself.

> Dazzling and tremendous how quick the sun-rise would kill me,
> If I could not now and always send sun-rise out of me.

He is able not only to "send sunrise" out of him but to speed like one of Harris' spirits through solar spheres: "I depart as air, I shake my locks at the runaway sun, / I effuse my flesh in eddies, and drift it in lacy jags." Like the Harmonialists, Whitman is not just appreciating nature but exhaling its magnetic force.

He was trying to define a model person who could heal both social and physical disease. The magnetic "I" at the heart of his poetry was the ideal Harmonial person, always ready to be absorbed into the mass but always himself—and, above all, in balance. Both spiritually and physically, the "I" is a Harmonial healer. "Of your soul I say truths to harmonize, if anything can harmonize you," he reassures us: Life is not "chaos or death—it is form, union, plan—it is eternal life—it is Happiness." "I shall be good health to you," he says at the end of "Song of Myself," "And filter and fibre your blood." In his 1855 poem "The Sleepers" the soothing "I" has all the capacities of a mesmeric healer and Harmonial life-affirmer. The poem moves through disease and social disorder to a sense of Harmonial peace.

It is not surprising, however, that it was the disordered, sometimes bizarre qualities of Whitman's verse that caught the eye of some reviewers, like one who noted that sometimes he ran toward chaos in rhapsodic time-space flights, "as in the rigmarole of trance-speaking mediums, and we are threatened on every hand with a period of mere suggestion in poetry, mere protest against order, and kicking at the old limits of time, space, the horizon, and the sky."[61] A British reviewer similarly pointed out that Whitman's time-space flights were odd to the foreign sensibility, "but perhaps not so to a nation from which the spirit-rappers sprung."[62]

Reviewers inclined to accept the new mystical movements, on the other hand, felt comfortable with Whitman's religious vision. The leading Harmonial journal of the 1850s, the *Christian Spiritualist*, gave a long, glowing review of the first edition of *Leaves of*

Grass, which it called "a sign of the times," representing a form of "poetic mediumship" that portrayed the influx of spirits and the divine breath.[63]

Although Whitman never joined any of the popular mystical movements, he remained curious about them to the end. Realizing they were a potent cultural force, he represented their spirit and their images in his all-absorbing poetry.

Six

SEX, GENDER, AND COMRADESHIP

DETERMINEDLY AVOIDING BOTH RETICENCE AND OBSCENITY, WHITMAN in his poetry brought to all kinds of love a fresh, passionate intensity. He profited from developments in the areas of physiology, marriage reform, and the visual arts.

Despite the sexual frankness of Whitman's poetry, he had a moralistic attitude toward pornography. Surveying the popular literature of the antebellum period, he said he saw "In the pleantiful [*sic*] feast of romance presented to us, all the novels, all the poems, really dish up only one figure, various forms and preparations of only one plot, namely, a sickly, scrofulous, crude amorousness." [1] In "Democratic Vistas" he complained that in "the prolific brood of the contemporary novel, magazine-tale, theatre-play, &c.," he found "the same endless thread of tangled and superlative love-story." [2] He was puzzled that some inferred from his poetry that he would take an interest in what he called "all the literature of rape, all the pornograph of vile minds." [3] He sharply distinguished *Leaves of*

Grass from this material: "No one would more rigidly keep in mind the difference between the simply erotic, the merely lascivious, and what is frank, free, modern, in sexual behavior, than I would: no one."

When it came to the content of popular literature, he was careful to praise morality and denounce obscenity. He attacked "the perfect cataracts of trash" produced by foreign sensational writers like Eugene Sue, Frederick Marryatt, William Harrison Ainsworth, and Charles Paul de Kock.[4] He was also dismayed when many American popular writers followed in the footsteps of the Europeans. In the wake of Eugene Sue's immensely popular exposé *The Mysteries of Paris* (1842–43), scores of lurid novels about the "mysteries" of American cities appeared. By 1857, in the *Daily Times*, Whitman could generalize: "Within the last ten or fifteen years a new school of literature has come into existence. We refer to what has aptly been called the 'sensation novel.'" So popular was this genre that he identified the love of sensationalism as America's leading characteristic: "If there be one characteristic of ourselves, as a people, more prominent than the others, it is our intense love of excitement. We must have our sensation, and we can no more do without it than the staggering inebriate can dispense with his daily dram."[5]

Although not explicit by today's standards, antebellum sensational fiction weirdly combined sex and violence and sometimes became daring, particularly in the hands of George Thompson, who churned out nearly a hundred pamphlet novels. Thompson dealt with all kinds of sex: group sex, child sex, miscegenation.

Given the popularity of sensational fiction, it is understandable that after Whitman's *Leaves of Grass* was criticized by some for its sexual openness, several of Whitman's defenders were quick to point out its relative purity when compared with the mass literature of the day. His friend William Douglas O'Connor asserted that the eighty or so sexual lines in Whitman did not merit his being lumped with "the anonymous lascivious trash spawned in holes and sold in corners, too witless and disgusting for any notice but that of the police."[6] Similarly, John Burroughs insisted, "Of the morbid, venereal, euphemistic, gentlemanly, club-house lust, which, under thin disguises, is in every novel and most of the poetry of our times, he has not the faintest word or thought—not the faintest whisper."[7]

Indeed, Whitman wrote his poems partly as a response to the popular love plot, with its fast young men and depraved women. In planning his sexual cluster of poems "Children of Adam" he specified in his notebook that he wanted to present "a fully-complete, well-developed, man, eld, bearded, swart, fiery" as "a more than rival of the youthful type-hero of novels and love poems."[8] Later on he wrote: "In my judgment it is strictly true that on the present supplies of imaginative literature—the current novels, tales, romances, and what is called 'poetry'—enormous in quantity and utterly unwholesome in quality, lies the responsibility, (a great part of it anyhow,) of the absence in modern society of a noble, stalwart, and healthy and maternal race of Women, and of a strong and dominant moral conscience."[9] "Romances," a popular equivalent of novels in his day, became a word of opprobrium in his lexicon. "Great genius and the people of these states must never be demeaned to romances," he declared in the 1855 preface.[10]

He incorporated his protest against romances into his poetry, as in "Song of the Exposition," where he wrote:

Away with old romance!

Away with novels, plots and plays of foreign courts,

Away with love-verses sugar'd in rhyme, the intrigues, amours
    of idlers,

Fitted for only banquets of the night where dancers to late
    music slide,

The unhealthy pleasures, extravagant dissipations of the few,

With perfumes, heat and wine, beneath the dazzling
    chandeliers.

He found a powerful weapon against the perfervid sensuality of romances in the natural approach to sex and the body offered by the ascendant science of physiology. Popular physiologists like those associated with the scientific publishing firm of Fowlers & Wells, distributor of the first edition of *Leaves of Grass* and publisher of the second, opposed pornography as one of several unnatural stimulants that threatened to disturb the mind's equilibrium by overexciting the brain's faculty of amativeness.

In one of their main books on physiology the Fowlers emphasized, "Though the world is *full* of books attempting to portray this passion [love]—though tales, novels, fictitious writings, love-stories, &c., by far the most numerous class of books, are made up, warp and woof, of love, . . . yet how imperfectly understood is this whole subject!" Such stories, he argued, made the brain's organ of amativeness overactive by exciting imaginary love. In another book, in an admonitory chapter on "Yellow Covered Literature," they unequivocally advised, "Read no love-stories unless you have health and sexuality to throw away."[11] The earliest publishers of the nineteenth century's most sexually frank poet, therefore, had a deep-seated hatred of the kind of scabrous popular literature he also denounced.

Whitman saw in the emerging class of popular physiological books on sex a healthy alternative to the prevalent lewdness of literature and conversation. In several best-selling works on physiology and phrenology Orson Fowler argued that married couples must have regular sex to keep their systems in balance. It was almost certainly Orson Fowler who was responsible for taking on *Leaves of Grass* as a Fowlers & Wells book in the mid-fifties, since by then his views on sex accorded almost exactly with Whitman's.

Both Orson Fowler and Whitman had a deep-seated belief in the sacredness and purity of sex when rightly treated. Both stood opposed to the desacralization of sex in popular culture, and both hoped to reinstate sex as fully natural, the absolute center of existence. In his book *Sexual Science* Fowler set out views on sex that were very close to Whitman's. Sex is to people, he wrote, "what steam power is to machinery—the prime instrumentality of its motions and productions," the very "chit-function of all males and females."[12] This was close in spirit to Whitman's poetic lines, "Sex contains all, bodies, souls, / [. . .]Without shame the man I like knows and avows the deliciousness of his sex, / Without shame the woman I like knows and avows hers."[13] Or, as Whitman later declared to Traubel, "Sex is the root of it all: sex—the coming together of men and women: sex: sex."[14]

With Fowler as with Whitman, all organs and acts connected with sex were holy. Both placed special emphasis on motherhood, the womb, the phallus, and semen. Just as Whitman in his poetry virtually deified mothers as initiators of life, so Fowler wrote, "She is the pattern woman who initiates the most life, while she who fails in this, fails in the very soul and essence of womanhood." Just as Whitman poeticized the folds of the womb whence unfolded new life, so Fowler praised the womb as "the vestibule of all life," insisting that "every iota of female beauty comes from it." Just as Whitman in "A Woman Waits for Me" would write that all is lacking in woman if sex is lacking, so Fowler underscored the necessity for woman's full enjoyment of the sex act. "PASSION ABSOLUTELY NECESSARY IN WOMAN," he headlined one section of his book. "The non-participant female," he wrote, "is a natural abomination." The outlook of both Fowler and Whitman was sex-based, womb-centered, phallic-centered, but also intensely religious. If Whitman's sexual passages often soar quickly to the mystical, so do Fowler's. For instance, the holiness Whitman saw in the "seminal milk" and "fatherstuff" was seen also by Fowler, who wrote of the semen, "Great God, what wonders hast Thou wrought by means of this infinitesimal sway!"[15]

Among the methods the physiologists used to educate the American public about the body and sex was the distribution of anatomical drawings and artistic prints. The Greek revival style that swept through American domestic architecture and cemetery design during this period was also manifested in the sculpture of Horatio Greenough and Hiram Powers. Greenough called for an honest treatment of the nude, and his call was heeded by a number of artists, including Hiram Powers. Powers' "The Greek Slave," a neoclassical study of a mournful, very naked slave woman whose chained hands fall strategically over the genital region, became the most famous American sculpture of the period. Other such vehicles were life-sized anatomical drawings of the nude human body, in color and on rollers, which Fowlers and Wells sold to schools and sometimes individuals.

Whitman saw in such aesthetic and scientific works a model for his poetic treatment of the body. "I prefer the honest nude to the suggestive half-draped," he would tell Traubel.[16] His attraction to the "honest nude" was stimulated in part by "The Greek Slave," which he thought even the most innocent could enjoy without being sullied. The aesthetic sensibility behind Powers' nude he also found in the "model artists," or *tableaux vivants*, which became the rage throughout the country in the late 1840s. In New Orleans he regularly attended model artist exhibitions, in which nude or lightly draped women and men enacted scenes from the Bible or classical myths. He denounced as "sickly prudishness" opposition to the model artists, which he thought revealed "Nature's cunningest work—the human frame, form and face."[17]

His interest in such public exhibitions of the nude informed his treatment of the body in his poetry. In the 1855 preface he described the healthy effects of reproducing artistic nudes: "Clean and vigorous children are jetted and conceived only in those communities where the models of natural forms are public every day."[18] He emphasized that Americans "shall receive no pleasure from violations of natural models" in sculptures or illustrations; specifically, "Of the human form especially it is so great it must never be made ridiculous." Such candid nudity was exemplified for him not only by sculptures and model artists but also by the physiologists' anatomical models. When planning in his notebook "a poem in which is minutely described the whole particulars and ensemble of a *first-rate Human Body*," he reminded himself: "Read the latest and best anatomical works/talk with physicians/study the anatomical plates."[19]

In his poetry he treated sex and the body in a physiological, artistic way as a contrast to what he saw as the cheapened, often perverse forms of sexual expression in popular culture. "Who will underrate the influence of a loose popular literature in debauching the popular mind?" he asked in a magazine article.[20] Directly opposing the often grotesque versions of eroticism appearing in sensational romances, he wrote in the 1855 preface: "Exaggerations will be sternly revenged in human physiology [...] As soon as histories are properly told, there is no more need for romances," a sentiment he repeated almost word for word in his 1860 poem "Suggestions."[21] Priding himself, like the physiologists, on candid acceptance of the body, he announced in his first poem: "Welcome is every organ and attribute of me, and of any man hearty and clean." He sang the naturalness of copulation and the sanctity of the sexual organs: "Perfect and clean the genitals previously jetting, perfect and clean the womb cohering."[22]

Whitman always emphasized the physiological connection. "I have always made much of the physiological," he once told Traubel.[23] After the first three editions prompted some adverse criticism because of their frankness, to ward off further attacks he wrote an opening poem, "Inscriptions," which placed his poetry in the clean realm of physiology:

Of physiology from top to toe I sing,
Not physiognomy alone nor brain alone is worthy
    for the Muse, I say the Form complete is worthier far,
The Female equally with the Male I sing.[24]

It is significant that these lines move quickly from physiological praise of the body to a feminist assertion of woman's equality, for in Whitman's mind the two subjects were interconnected. "[O]nly when sex is properly treated, talked, avowed, accepted," he wrote, "will the woman be equal with the man, and pass where the man passes, and meet his words with her words, and his rights with her rights."[25] With women's rights activists of the day he shared a concern for the right of woman to equal opportunity in society. Like advocates of free love, he thought relationships must be based on mutual attraction and respect rather than on money or one-sided desire.

For Whitman, there was great power and creativity in both motherhood and fatherhood. He was surrounded by physiologists who believed, in Orson Fowler's words, that "PARENTAGE is EVERYTHING."[26] Whitman deified the womb as the emblem of almost divine power. He writes of women, "[Y]our privilege encloses the rest, and is the exit of the rest, / You are the gates of the body, and you are the gates of the soul."[27] His 1856 poem "Unfolded Out of the Folds" sang praise to both the literal and metaphorical powers of the womb:

> Unfolded out of the folds of the woman man comes unfolded,
> and is always to come unfolded,
> Unfolded only out of the superbest woman of the earth is to
> come the superbest man of the earth, [...]
> Unfolded out of the strong and arrogant woman I love, only
> thence can appear the strong and arrogant man I love,
> Unfolded by brawny embraces from the well-muscled woman I
> love, only thence come the brawny embraces of the man, [...]
> First the man is shaped in the woman, he can then be shaped in
> himself.[28]

Whitman's poetic paeans to what he called "sane athletic maternity" are explainable as attempts to present a model woman for all to observe. In establishing this model, he drew off several emerging theories of womanhood. One was related to the athletic woman.

Such athletic prescriptions for women were common during a period when what has been called a cult of "Real Womanhood" was coming to the fore in American life and letters. The Real

Woman, although strong and economically self-reliant, believed in marriage and opposed political feminism. Whitman's poetry was one of the period's clearest expressions of the Real Woman: athletic, sturdy, self-reliant yet also maternal, family-based. Given the ideal of the Real Woman, there was no contradiction between the athletic and motherly roles he praised in his poetry. The woman in "Unfolded Out of the Folds," for instance, embodies tender maternal "sympathy" but also is "strong and arrogant," "well muscled," and capable of "brawny embraces." Another Whitman poem praised women who "know how to swim, row, ride, wrestle, shoot, run, strike, retreat, advance, resist, defend themselves."

Whitman also learned much from the women's rights movement, which became active and visible in America between 1848 and 1855, just when he was maturing as a poet. The world's first women's rights convention was held at Seneca Falls, New York in July 1848. Whitman once declared that *Leaves of Grass* was "essentially a woman's book, . . . it is the cry of the right and the wrong of the woman sex."[29] It was so, in the most far-ranging sense.

With his background in Quakerism and freethought, Whitman was predisposed to respond to the women's rights movement. He was a close observer of woman's oratory and became a poetic celebrant of woman's new public role. He had especially high regard for the feminist orators Fanny Wright, Lucretia Mott, and Ernestine Rose.

Women participated in parades, processions, and religious revivals in unprecedented numbers during this period. Whitman approvingly recorded woman's suddenly public posture in "Song of the Broad-Axe," picturing a city "Where women walk in public processions in the streets the same as the men, / Where they enter the public assembly and take places the same as the men."[30]

Before the Civil War, women's rights activism centered on property-holding, education, employment, and marriage. It was these issues that would always loom largest in Whitman's mind. He was painfully aware of what happened to a woman's wages or property holdings in marriage: They were turned over to the husband. In marriage, early-nineteenth-century American women forfeited their legal and economic existence

He watched with fascinated yet sometimes puzzled interest in the various reforms that arose in response to flawed relations between the sexes. Antebellum America was an extremely fertile breeding ground for various religious and secular groups who practiced alternative lifestyles in an effort to put sexual relations on an entirely new basis. At one extreme were the Shakers, who practiced celibacy, at the other were free lovers, who called for the abolishment of marriage and the reestablishment of relationships on the basis of "passional attraction."

Free love was the most pertinent of these movements with regard to Whitman. Between 1850 and 1855 America witnessed the formation of two free love communities, at Modern Times, New York and at Berlin Heights, Ohio, as well as various free love clubs, journals, societies. At Modern Times, an anarchist and free love community established in 1851 near Whitman's birthplace on Long Island, legal marriage was abolished. Couples signified their union by tying a colored thread on their finger and took it off when the passion fizzled.

Free love was a direct response to what was seen as the enslaving marriage institution. Free love writers such as Marx Edgeworth Lazarus and Stephen Pearl Andrews argued that marriage in America had become little more than legalized prostitution. But the free lovers did not emphasize promiscuity. Free love for them did not mean indiscriminate love but love freely given, freely shared. The precondition for sexual relations should be love, not marriage, and the woman should determine when sex took place. Thus the free lovers, though often castigated, considered themselves chaste and pure.

The association between Whitman and free love was often made in his day. Emerson connected him with the free love movement, as did James Harlan, Whitman's superior in the Interior Department who in 1865 fired him, reportedly, in the belief that he "was a free lover, deserved punishment, &c."[31] When the 1881 edition of *Leaves of Grass* was banned in Boston, it was the New England Free Love League that publicly came to Whitman's defense and endorsed his sexual poetry.

Still, Whitman was ambivalent about the free lovers. Like them, he saw profound defects in relations between the sexes that he tried to repair by appealing to natural passion and attraction. But he shied away from what he saw as the free lovers' potentially disruptive effects on society. Despite his own disinclination to marry and his recognition of flaws in American marriages, he always venerated the marriage institution. "When that goes, all goes," he wrote, emphasizing that "the divine institution of the marriage tie lies at the root of the welfare, the safety, the very existence of every Christian nation."[32]

What he wanted was the "passional" theory of the free lovers without their anti-marriage proposals. It was the poetry in the first three editions of *Leaves of Grass*, written when passional theory was at its peak of cultural influence, that the discourse of magnetic attraction was most pronounced. The gravity-like pull between humans expounded by Fourier and disseminated by the American reformers is felt at many moments in Whitman's poetry. "Crossing Brooklyn Ferry" asks: "What is more subtle than this which ties me to the woman or man that looks in my face? / Which fuses me into you now, and pours my meaning into you?"[33] Sometimes his vocabulary of attraction seems straight out of passional theory:

O to attract by more than attraction!
How it is I know not—yet behold! the something which obeys
    none of the rest,
It is offensive, never defensive—yet how magnetic it draws.

Just as the free lovers had discovered in passional attraction a human counterpart to the earth's gravity, so Whitman wrote:

I am he that aches with amorous love;
Does the earth gravitate? does not all matter, aching, attract all
    matter?
So the body of me to all I meet or know.

Self-determination in sexual matters was the notion that free lovers had in common with many feminists and with Whitman. The reason the free lovers called marriage legalized prostitution was their vision of countless wives bound by law to husbands whom they detested and yet who had free access to their bodies. When Whitman in "A Woman Waits for Me" says that all is lacking in a woman if the moisture of "the right man" is lacking, he was advancing the idea of self-choice for women.

All the flaws in relations between the sexes could be seen in that most public form of sex in antebellum America: prostitution. Whitman emphasized in his journalism that economic injustices against working women drove many of them to streetwalking. Sex was for sale everywhere in America's larger cities, especially New

York. Whitman noted in 1857 that nineteen of twenty urban men "are more or less familiar with houses of prostitution and are customers to them." Among "the best classes of Men" in the New York area, he wrote, "the custom is to go among prostitutes as an ordinary thing. Nothing is thought of it—or rather the wonder is, how can there be any 'fun' without it."[34]

Like others, he was appalled by the way prostitution was conducted in New York. In his walks about the city he reported seeing both the "notorious courtesan taking a 'respectable' promenade" and the "tawdry, hateful, foul-tongued, harsh-voiced harlots." To prevent the spread of disease and crime, he thought, prostitution should be regulated; he even suggested legalization.

A good first step was full exposure of the problem and the cultivation of a sympathetic public attitude toward prostitutes. The prevailing attitude was one of derogation and censure. A kindlier attitude toward them emerged in moral reform circles and among the physiologists Whitman read. "Abandoned females are generally considered as constitutionally the scum and offscouring of mankind," wrote Orson Fowler in 1851. "But are they not human beings? Perhaps as good by nature as ourselves."[35]

One of Whitman's aims in his poetry was to extend a generous hand to the victims of deceitful men. In the 1855 preface he refers to the "serpentine poison of those that seduce women" and in a poem he mentions "the treacherous seducer of young women."[36] As for prostitutes themselves, his poems made compassionate gestures toward them. His first picture of a prostitute, in the 1855 version of "Song of Myself," retained traces of his revulsion but tried to communicate sympathy:

> The prostitute draggles her shawl, her bonnet bobs on her
> tipsy and pimpled neck,

The crowd laugh at her blackguard oaths, the men jeer and
   wink to each other,
(Miserable! I do not laugh at your oaths nor jeer you;).

In later portraits he moved toward personal identification with
them: "You prostitutes flaunting over the troittoirs or obscene in
your rooms, / Who am I that I should call you more obscene than
myself?"

His most famous sympathetic gesture was his 1860 poem "To
a Common Prostitute":

Be composed—be at ease with me—I am Walt Whitman, liberal
   and lusty as Nature,
Not till the sun excludes you do I exclude you,
Not till the waters refuse to glisten for you and the leaves to rustle
   for you, do my words refuse to glisten and rustle for you.

My girl I appoint with you an appointment, and I charge you
   that you make preparation to be worthy to meet me,
And I charge you that you be patient and perfect till I come.

Till then I salute you with a significant look that you do not
   forget me.

The emphasis has shifted from the massive social problem that
appalled Whitman to the poetic solution, embodied in refreshing
nature images (the sun, the glistening waters) and the atmosphere
of dignity and formality ("be worthy to meet me," "be patient and
perfect," "I salute you with a significant look"). This "appointment"
with a prostitute was an ennobling one in which both parties profited, the "I" practicing democratic compassion, the prostitute being treated as a person rather than as a sex machine. Whitman gives

a modern version of Christ's compassionate treatment of Mary Magdalene by fusing democratic sympathy with images of beauty and ennoblement.

Culling positive, sympathetic attitudes toward sex, the body, and women from various cultural arenas, he presented powerful images which, when taken together, created a sexual program that held up the possibility of woman's social and personal liberation. The woman question preoccupied Whitman from the start:

> I am the poet of the woman the same as the man,
>
> And I say it is as great to be a woman as to be a man,
>
> And I say there is nothing greater than the mother of men.[37]

In Whitman's day, women's rights and motherhood were not necessarily contradictory. The feminist leader Elizabeth Cady Stanton was a devoted wife and mother who took pleasure in housekeeping. Several women in Whitman's circle, such as Paulina Wright Davis and Nelly O'Connor, were at once feminists and housekeepers. Without fear of contradiction, then, Whitman could praise simultaneously the ideas of motherhood and women's equality. His pronouncements on equality of the sexes can sound at once feminist and familial:

> The wife, and she is not one jot less than the husband,
>
> The daughter, and she is just as good as the son,
>
> The mother, and she is every bit as much as the father.

He was repelled by the single-minded focus of certain feminists on individual issues. For instance, when he wrote in 1876 that he stood for "the radical equality of the sexes, (not at all for the 'woman's rights' point of view, however)," he seems to have been distancing himself from groups like Lucy Stone's American Woman Suffrage Association, which by then focused solely on winning the vote for women.[38]

Whitman believed women's equality could be gained only after wholesale changes in relations between the sexes. He created in his poetry a utopian space where such relations are restored to dignity and mutual respect. Minimized in his poems are the flaws in gender relations he perceived all around him: declining health and fertility among women; trickery and misogyny on the part of men; legal discrimination against women; mockery of prostitutes; the contrasting extremes of prudish repressiveness and pornographic lasciviousness. Maximized are physiological acceptance of the body and sex; fertility and athleticism; and an all-pervasive passional attraction.

His poem "A Woman Waits for Me" brings together a number of these elements: a frank recognition of women's sexual nature; admiration of the Real Woman, who can row, wrestle, shoot, and so on; a feminist claim that women "are not one jot less than I am"; and an endorsement of sexual self-determination and passional attraction, enforced in the lines about women who are aroused only by "the right man" and who "refuse to awake at the touch of any man but me."[39]

To his frustration, his candid treatment of sex enraged the moral censors of his era. Those who espoused the prudish view of sex did not approve of his sexual images, no matter how much he tried to couch them in religious or physiological language. When a British edition of *Leaves of Grass* appeared in 1868, the editors carefully pruned away sexual references, producing an expurgated edition. Publication of the 1881 edition was suspended by the

Boston district attorney on the grounds that it violated public statutes concerning obscene literature. (The phrase "banned in Boston" came from this episode.)

It tells us a lot about sexual mores of the time that these priggish censors complained of even the mildest references to heterosexual sex while finding nothing objectionable in Whitman's numerous images of same-sex love. Amazingly, the 1881 censors targeted even the tame "Dalliance of the Eagles" (about the mating of birds) while leaving untouched all but one of the homoerotic "Calamus" poems—and in that one, "Spontaneous Me," it was images of masturbation and copulation, not homoerotic ones, that were called obscene.

Why were the "Calamus" poems, widely viewed today as homosexual love songs, permitted to stand by these exacting, puritanical readers? The answer is that same-sex love was not interpreted the same way then as it is now.

Passionate intimacy between people of the same sex was common in pre–Civil War America. The lack of clear sexual categories (homo-, hetero-, bi-) made same-sex affection unself-conscious and widespread. Although Whitman evidently had one or two affairs with women, he was mainly a romantic comrade who had a series of intense relationships with young men, most of whom went on to get married and have children. Whatever the nature of his physical relationships with them, most of the passages of same-sex love in his poems were not out of keeping with then-current theories and practices that underscored the healthiness of such love.

Same-sex friends often loved each other passionately. "Lover" had no gender connotation and was used interchangeably with "friend." Thus Emerson could call his friends "excellent lovers,

Whitman in the late 1860s. *Ed Folsom Collection*

who carry out the world for me to new and noble depths."[40] Similarly, Whitman in a "Calamus" poem wrote, "And when I thought
how my dear friend, my lover, was on his way coming, O then I was
happy."[41] The word "orgy" had no sexual connotation; it meant
"party." When Whitman writes, "I share the midnight orgies of

young men," or imagines a "city of orgies" where "lovers, con-
tinual lovers, only repay me," he is imaginatively participating in
the uninhibited gatherings that working-class comrades enjoyed.[42]

It was common among both men and women to hug, kiss, and
express love for people of the same sex. In hotels and inns, complete strangers often slept in the same bed. Neither "to sleep with"
nor "to make love to" had the sexual meanings they would take
on in the 1890s. In "Behold This Swarthy Face" Whitman typically writes: "Yet comes one a Manhattanese and ever at parting
kisses me on the lips with robust love, / [. . .] We observe that
salute of American comrades land and sea, / We are those two
natural and nonchalant persons."

Because Whitman was disillusioned with the capitalistic forces
that poisoned many heterosexual relationships, producing rampant prostitution as well as "legalized prostitution" in marriage,
he wished to glorify the loving friendship he saw around him in
working-class life. He said in his notebook that he wanted to find
words for the "approval, admiration, friendship" seen "among
young men of these States," who he said had "wonderful tenacity
of friendship, and passionate fondness for their friends."[43] He
wanted to be the one who brought real-life friendship to the
printed page. As he wrote in his open letter to Emerson, "as to
manly friendship, everywhere observed in These States, there is
not the first breath of it to be observed in print."[44]

The phrenological notion of adhesiveness was an important
element of his view of comradeship. His friends the Fowlers wrote
that when the organ of adhesiveness was well developed, one
"loves friends with tenderness" and "will sacrifice almost anything
for their sake." Orson Fowler wrote that those with large adhe-

siveness "instinctively recognize it in each other; soon become mutually and strongly attached; desire to cling to the objects of their love; take more delight in the exercise of friendship than in anything else."[45] Adhesiveness had a personal and social dimension. Privately it caused people of the same sex to be drawn to each other and love each other. Socially, it was a powerful force for cohesion, with the power, as the Fowlers wrote, to "bind mankind together in families, societies, communities, &c."

When planning the clusters of poems for the 1860 edition of his volume, Whitman specified that the "Children of Adam" poems would embody the "amative love of women" while "Calamus" represented "adhesiveness, manly love."[46] In one "Calamus" poem he wrote, "I announce adhesiveness—I say it shall be limitless, unloosened."[47] In another he declared, "O adhesiveness! O pulse of my life!"

The social dimension of comradeship was crucial to him as well. When discussing the "Calamus" poems with Traubel he explained that comradely love "is one of the United States—it is the quality which makes the states whole—it is their thread—but oh! The significant thread—by which the nation is held together, a chain of comrades . . . I know no country anyhow in which comradeship is so far developed as here—here, among the mechanic classes."[48] In the 1876 preface to his poems he wrote, "the special meaning of the 'Calamus' cluster of 'Leaves of Grass' . . . mainly resides in its political significance," adding that it was through "the beautiful and same affection of man for men, latent in all the young fellows, north and south, east and west" that the United States "are to be most effectually welded together, intercalcated, anneal'd into a living union."[49]

It is understandable that he made this political application of friendship with special fervor in the 1860 edition. Talk of a forthcoming "irrepressible conflict" filled the air. Lincoln had recently warned, "A house divided against itself cannot stand." Since Whitman had lost faith in established institutions, he looked to friendship to unify his nation. The calamus plant, a tall, fragrant reed that grows by ponds and rivers, was a convenient metaphor. Its marginality reflected Whitman's attempt to remove himself from mainstream institutions; its pungent odor symbolized the beauty and pervasiveness of the comradeship he hoped would replace these institutions.

His hope for unifying his nation through loving comradeship is expressed in several "Calamus" poems, including one that asks, "States! / Were you looking to be held together by lawyers? / By an agreement on paper? Or by arms? / Away! . . . There shall be from me a new friendship" that "shall circulate through The States" and "twist and intertwist them through and around each other," as "Affection shall solve everyone of the problems of freedom."[50] Through friendship,

> I will make the continent indissoluble,
> I will make the most splendid race the sun ever shone upon,
> I will make divine magnetic lands.[51]

Friendship, he said hopefully, "will make the continent indissoluble." Less than a year after these words were printed, the nation would be at war.

Seven

THE CIVIL WAR, LINCOLN, AND RECONSTRUCTION

CIVIL WAR WAS NOT WHAT WHITMAN HAD WANTED OR EXPECTED, BUT it turned out to be what he needed—and, he came to believe, what the nation needed. "My book and the war are one," he said in a poem.[1] In the 1876 preface he explained: "The whole book, indeed, revolves around that four years' war, which, as I was in the midst of it, becomes, in 'Drum Taps,' pivotal to the rest entire."[2]

In his view, the Civil War accomplished what he had hoped his poetry would accomplish. It blew away many of the social ills that his early poetry had tried to rectify. It cleared the atmosphere like a thunderstorm. It seemed to rid the North, especially Manhattan, of many of its prewar problems. It turned the fuzzy, shifting issue of states' rights versus national power into the crystal-clear one of Secession versus Union. It made most of the people in the North rally around the ideal of union he had long cherished. It pulled together virtually all Americans, North and South, in a common action and a spirit of heroic self-sacrifice.

Whitman got an intimate look at the war through his brother George, who joined a Brooklyn regiment in June 1861 and three months later signed on with the Fifty-first New York Volunteers under Colonel Edward Ferrero. Over the next four years George traveled more than twenty thousand miles and was in twenty-one engagements or sieges. Constantly under fire, he gave vivid accounts of the war in his letters home. Stolidly courageous, he received several promotions. Not only did George send home reports of his experiences, but his being wounded at Fredericksburg was what drew Walt to the front and then to Washington, where he nursed thousands of soldiers in the war hospitals.

In an essay called "The Origins of Attempted Secession" Whitman insisted "the Northern States . . . were really just as responsible for that war . . . as the South." He explained that in the North, "especially in New York and Philadelphia cities," the political system was becoming "composed of more and more putrid and dangerous materials," of disunionists, infidels, "pimpled men," "scarred men," "skeletons," and so on. "Is it strange, he asked, that thunderstorm follow'd such morbid and stifling cloud strata?"[3]

He saw the war as a necessary cleansing agent. His new poems reflected his exultation:

> War! An arm'd race is advancing! the welcome for battle, no
> turning away;
> War! Be it weeks, months, or years, an arm'd race is advancing
> to welcome it.

The hard certainty of war appealed to him. Sometimes he manifested an almost masochistic delight in the violence, as in the uncollected poem "Ship of Libertad":

Blow mad winds!
Rage, boil, vex, yawn wide, yeasty waves
Crash away [...]

Welcome the storm—welcome the trial—[...]
I welcome the menace—I welcome thee with joy.[4]

Since he thought the North needed purifying as much as the South, several of his poems pictured the war as cleansing the Augean stables of capitalism and urbanism. In "First O Songs for a Prelude" he describes the lawyer, the driver, the judge, and others of various economic backgrounds melding as armed regiments. "How good they look as they tramp down to the river, sweaty, with their guns on their shoulders!"[5] In "Beat! Beat! Drums!" the war is a "ruthless force" that bursts through everything and wrenches people from their peacetime pursuits. The inspiriting music of war blows "through the windows—through doors," scattering the congregation, the scholars, the merchants engaged in their capitalist double-dealing: "No bargainers' bargains by day—no brokers or speculators—would they continue?"[6]

So important was the war and its violence to his imagination that he would devote a disproportionate section of his autobiography *Specimen Days* to the war years. Part of the reason for this lies in what Whitman saw as the war's purgative violence. "The real war will never get into the books," he wrote, referring to "the seething hell and the black infernal background of countless minor scenes and interiors."[7] It was the sheer tumult and adventure of the war that he registered in *Specimen Days*.

He captured the hell of war in some of the poems in *Drum-Taps*, such at "The Artilleryman's Vision":

I hear the sounds of the different missiles, the short *t-h-t! t-h-t!*
    of the rifle-balls,
I see the shells exploding leaving small white clouds, I hear the
    great shrieking shells as they pass, [. . .]
And even the sound of the cannon far or near, (rousing even in
    dreams a devilish exultation and all the old mad joy in the
    depths of my soul.)[8]

It was during his long hours as a volunteer nurse in Washington's hospitals that he saw the results of the war's violence with special vividness. The suffering he witnessed in the hospitals was on a scale unmatched in American history. More Americans died and were wounded in the Civil War than in all other wars *combined*. Whitman filled his notebooks and letters with descriptions of soldiers afflicted with virtually every imaginable wound or with maladies like diarrhea and dysentery. He recorded his hospital visits in his poem "The Wound-Dresser":

To the long rows of cots up and down each side I return,
To each and all one after another I draw near, not one do I miss,
An attendant follows holding a tray, he carries a refuse pail,
Soon to be fill'd with clotted rags and blood, emptied, and
    filled again.[9]

Like other aspects of the war, his hospital visits accomplished key things he had hoped his poetry would do. They validated his vision of the common man; they answered his need for an ideal family and loving comrades; and they permitted full indulgence of his humanistic, magnetic medical ideas. He had filled the first three editions of *Leaves of Grass* with fresh, Adamic common people whose goodness or picturesqueness was intended to counteract the governmental corruption that had contributed to the political crisis of the fifties. When he settled in Washington, he found that something wonderful was happening: the capital city was being flooded by young men—the wounded in the hospitals—who were accomplishing the very social cleansing he had designed his poetry to do. To Emerson he wrote of his plan to write a "little book" about "this phase of America: her masculine young manhood, . . . her fair youth—brought and deposited here in this great, whited sepulchre of Washington (this union Capital without the first bit of cohesion—this collect of proofs how low and swift a good stock can deteriorate—)." He exulted that Providence had brought to this sink of political corruption a "freight of helpless worn and wounded youth, genuine of the soil, . . . of the first unquestioned and convincing western crop, prophetic of the future, proofs undeniable to all men's ken of perfect beauty, tenderness and pluck that never race rivall'd."[10]

The soldiers he saw in the hospitals, he would say later, saved him and saved America by displaying all the qualities he associated with ideal humanity. Before the war, he had fallen into a deep cynicism about American society that his hospital experiences eradicated. As he told Traubel: "There were years in my life—years there in New York—when I wondered if all were not going bad with America—the tendency downwards—but the war saved me: what I saw in the war set me up for all time—the days in the hospitals." He said he was thinking of "not chiefly the facts of battles, marches, what-not—but the social being-ness of the soldiers" in the hospitals.[11] Generosity, tact, propriety, affection, and, always, toughness in the face of suffering and death: these were the qualities he saw among the wounded. "Not a bit of sentimentalism or whining have I seen about a single death-bed in hospital or on the field, but generally impassive indifference."[12]

Patients in Armory Square Hospital, one of the military hospitals in Washington, D.C. Whitman frequented during the Civil War.
Library of Congress, Prints and Photographs Division

He took on the role as the comforting, pious wound dresser embracing the heroic, helpless soldiers. In "Vigil Strange I Kept on the Field One Night" he gave his version of the emotional battlefield death, a common theme of the day. The poem mixes wartime violence, comradely love, and patriotic piety, as a soldier sits up all night with a mortally wounded comrade, devoting "immortal and mystic hours" to his "son of responding kisses" whom he says he will meet in heaven.[13] In "A March in the Ranks Hard-Prest" he gives the grisly details of the death of a young soldier to whom he affectionately tends until he is called to join his marching regiment.

Although Whitman still saw corruption in the government, during the war he considered subordinate officials corrupt but the higher ones, especially President Lincoln, basically sound.

Whitman admired Lincoln from the start of the war. Just as Lincoln said early on that he was pursuing the war to preserve the

Union rather than extirpate slavery, so Whitman was fixated on the idea of Union. Having long hated both Abolitionists and fire-eaters because they threatened to destroy the Union, Whitman was delighted when the war brought things to a head. "By that war," he said, "*exit* fire-eaters, *exit* Abolitionists."[14] The South's greatest sin, he thought, was secession; the North's greatest virtue was devotion to the Union. Lincoln, weaned in the Henry Clay school of nationality, epitomized this virtue above all. Whitman declared of Lincoln that "UNIONISM, in its truest and amplest sense, form'd the hard-pan of his character."[15]

Whitman saw Lincoln some twenty to thirty times in Washington. He didn't meet the president, but saw him riding through the city for business or pleasure. "I see the President almost every day," he wrote in the summer of 1863. "We have got so that we exchange bows, and very cordial ones." Once Lincoln gave Whitman a long stare. "He has a face like a Hoosier Michel Angelo," Whitman wrote, "so awful ugly it becomes beautiful, with its strange mouth, its deep cut, criss-cross lines, and its doughnut complexion."[16]

Abraham Lincoln. *Miriam and Ira D. Wallach Division of Art, Prints and Photographs, The New York Public Library*

No other human being seemed as multifaceted to Whitman as Lincoln. The president, he said, had "canny shrewdness" and "*horse-sense.*" He seemed the down-home, average American, with his drab looks and his humor, redolent of barnyards and barrooms. Whitman commented on the "somewhat rusty and dusty appearance" of Lincoln, who "looks about as ordinary in attire, &c., as the commonest man." Whitman was excited that "the commonest average of life—a railsplitter and a flat-boatsman!"—now occupied the presidency.[17]

Funny and unaffected, Lincoln nonetheless had, Whitman wrote, "a deep latent sadness in the expression." He was "every easy, flexible, tolerant, almost slouch, respecting the minor matters" but capable of "indomitable firmness (even obstinacy) on rare occasions, involving great points." He was a family man but was had an air of complete independence: "He went his own lonely road," Whitman said, "disregarding all the usual ways—refusing the guides, accepting no warnings—just keeping his appointment with himself every time." His "composure was marvellous" in the face of unpopularity and great difficulties during the war. He had what Whitman saw as a profoundly religious quality. His "mystical foundations" were "mystical, abstract, moral and spiritual," and his "religious nature" was "of the amplest, deepest-rooted, loftiest kind." Summing Lincoln up, Whitman called him "the greatest, best, most characteristic, artistic, moral personality" in American life.[18]

In short, Lincoln, as Whitman saw him, was virtually the living embodiment of the "I" of *Leaves of Grass*. He was "one of the roughs" but also, for Whitman, "a kosmos," with the whole range of qualities that term implied. If, as Whitman said, *Leaves of Grass* and the war were one, they particularly came together in Lincoln.

As impressive as Lincoln was in life, it was his death that for Whitman was the crucial, transcendent moment in American history. John Wilkes Booth's murder of Lincoln in Washington's Ford Theatre on April 14, 1865 was, in Whitman's view, a culminating moment for America. There was good reason Whitman would give his "Death of Abraham Lincoln" speech over and over again in the last dozen years of his life. He became fixated on what he called "the tragic splendor of [Lincoln's] death, purging, illuminating all."[19] The assassination, he declared, had unequalled influence on the shaping of the Republic.

Many violent, contradictory cultural elements Whitman had tried to harness and redirect in *Leaves of Grass* found their outlet in the tragic event that he would always believe offered a model for social unification. In Lincoln's death, he declared, "there is a cement to the whole people, subtler, more underlying, than any thing written in constitution, or courts or armies." The reminiscence of Lincoln's death, he noted, "belongs to these States in their entirety—not the North only, but the South—perhaps belongs most tenderly and devotedly to the South," the president's birthplace.[20] In death, Lincoln became the Martyr Chief, admired by many of his former foes.

Lincoln had, in Whitman's view, accomplished the cleansing and unifying mission he had designed for *Leaves of Grass*. It is not surprising that Whitman's writing changed dramatically after the Civil War. Never again would he write all-encompassing poems like "Song of Myself" or "The Sleepers," for he believed that Lincoln and the war had encompassed all cultural materials.

In Whitman's best-known poems about Lincoln, "O Captain! My Captain!" and "When Lilacs Last in the Dooryard Bloom'd," the silencing of his former poetic self is noticeable. Both poems marginalize Whitman and concentrate on Lincoln, presaging the poet's obsession with Lincoln in late years. In "O Captain!" the fixation is visible in the image of the "I" staring relentlessly at Lincoln's bloody, pale corpse on the ship of state's deck amid celebrations heralding the ship's return to port. In "Lilacs" Lincoln is the majestic western star, while the poet is the wood thrush, the "shy and hidden bird" singing of death with a "bleeding throat."[21] No longer does Whitman's brash "I" present himself as the Answerer or arouse readers with a "barbaric yawp." In the war and Lincoln, many of the nation's most pressing problems had reached painful resolution, changing the poet's role from that of America's imaginary leader to that of eulogist of its actual leader.

Although Lincoln and the war would always be transcendent ideals for Whitman, he had to face the fact that the ideals were not

Whitman's handwritten revision to "O Captain! My Captain!"
Library of Congress, Prints and Photographs Division

matched by the realities of postbellum America. Industrialization and the growth of new power structures brought new challenges for the poet intent on social salvation.

The war remained a retrospective touchstone for Whitman. It was, he wrote, "the Verteber of Poetry and Art, (of personal character too,) for all future America."[22] But he found that the ideal nation made possible by the war was not mirrored by the reality of postbellum America. Neither the war nor his poetry had purified the political atmosphere. The Tweed Ring, the Crédit Mobilier, and other sordid operations, leading to the notorious corruption of Grant's administration, made Whitman believe, on some level, that America's problems were more dire than ever.

But he was more confident than before that these problems would disappear with time. He regained faith in the democratic political process, and he got philosophical consolation from an intensified belief in Hegelianism and progressive evolution. With his poetic "I" no longer able to absorb and recycle massive amounts of cultural material, his poems became, principally, brief vignettes or thoughts, as though his imagination had surrendered an all-encompassing posture on behalf of writing for the occasion. His change from rebellious individualist to Good Gray Poet was played out against the background of the rise of corporate capitalism and institutional organizations.

Before the war, his temperament and poetry had reflected a free-flowing culture with few centralized institutions. After the war, with the rise of big business and a strong federal government, such institutions confronted him, and much of his later life was defined by them. He faced a new repressiveness in sexual matters, evidenced by his being fired by the Interior Department in 1865 and later by the government-authorized Comstockery that lay behind the banning of the 1881 edition of *Leaves of Grass*. Although designed to suppress Whitman, these institutional actions actually aided his cause by arousing the loyalty of his followers and increasing his visibility. Ironically, the institutions aimed against him helped make him a cultural institution.

Much of his fame late in life rested on his firing from the government by the Secretary of the Interior, James Harlan. When Whitman friend William Douglas O'Connor took revenge against Harlan by writing his pamphlet *The Good Gray Poet*, he gave rise to what might be called the Whitman Myth: the image of the poet as a neglected genius who was thoroughly patriotic, personally exemplary, and almost spotless in his writings. Versions of this sanitized image would be pounded home time and again for the rest of Whitman's life, by the poet himself and by others.

If Whitman's public image became more conservative after the war, so, in some respects, did his private attitudes. He was a strong supporter of President Andrew Johnson, a white-supremacist who was lenient toward the South. Whitman said Johnson had "an inherent integrity" and opposed the president's foes in Congress, the Radical Republicans.[23] Whitman's job in the attorney general's office between July 1865 and January 1872 initially involved enforcing Johnson's most controversial policy: granting pardons to former rebels.

How could Whitman possibly support the reactionary Johnson while damning the Radical Republicans and other supporters of civil rights? Like Whitman, Johnson was devoted simultaneously to the Union and to states' rights. As president, he was concerned mainly not with retribution but with restoring the Union by respecting the wishes of the individual Southern states.

Whitman, more worried than ever about the balance between the individual and the mass, felt this balance was more closely approached by Johnson than by the Radical Republicans. In *Notes Left Over* Whitman reiterated a long-standing conviction about the essence of America: "There are two distinct principles—aye, paradoxes—at the life-fountain of the States: one, the sacred principle of Union, the right of ensemble, at whatever sacrifice—and yet another, an equally sacred principle, the right of each State, consider'd as a separate sovereign individual, in its own sphere." Either "the centrifugal law" alone or "the centripetal law" alone, he stressed, would be fatal to the nation.[24] Johnson combined an old-fashioned states' rights view with a Lincolnish, pro-Union one.

So important was this balancing of the individual and the mass that he introduced the 1867 *Leaves of Grass* and all later editions with a poem that in its final version began:

One's-Self I sing, a simple separate person,
Yet utter the word Democratic, the word En-Masse.[25]

Seeking metaphors for the right balance became almost an obsession in his later years, but he could no longer rely on an all-powerful poetic "I" to achieve the balance. He seemed to find a "solution of the paradox" everywhere but in himself. He found it in a future race of "bards," in New York City, in the railroad, in the Mississippi River basin, and in the geography and people of the American West, to name a few phenomena he discussed this way.

Whitman's racial views took a conservative turn after the war. During the 1850s, he had shared the fervent racial egalitarianism of Frederick Douglass, Samuel Ringgwold Ward, and others who called attention to the humanity and nobility of African Americans.

Whitman has rightly been cherished as a great spokesperson for racial brotherhood and equality.

But this message was far more prominent in his pre–Civil War poems than in his later ones. Whitman admired the African Americans who had served in the Union army. But he was unequipped to ponder the legal and political ramifications of emancipation. Whitman never said much about African American suffrage, but when he did, his remarks were derogatory. In an essay on the suffrage he sounded both nativist and racist: "As if we had not strained the voting and digestive caliber of American Democracy to the utmost fort the last fifty years with the millions of ignorant foreigners, we have now infused a powerful percentage of blacks, with about as much intellect and calibre (in the mass) as so many baboons."[26]

His racism was fueled by the so-called "ethnological science" of the era which held that certain "inferior" races would disappear as a result of natural selection. He would tell Traubel: "The nigger, like the Injun, will be eliminated: it is the law of the race, history, what-not: always so far inexorable—always to be. Someone proves that a superior grade of rats comes and then all the minor rats are cleared out."[27] These views, deeply unsettling, were common in his time. A recent historian of science affirms that "the belief in the Negro's extinction became one of the most pervasive ideas in American medical and anthropological thought during the late nineteenth century."[28] Whitman, with his amateurish but ardent respect of science, bought into ethnography.

His 1871 essay "Democratic Vistas" revealed that within six years after the war had ended, his disillusion over materialism and corruption had returned. Surveying American society, he wrote: "The spectacle is appalling. . . . The depravity of the business classes of our country is not less than it has been supposed, but infinitely greater." He added that "the official services of America," state and federal, "are saturated in corruption, bribery, falsehood, and mal-administration."[29] However, he had gained a new source of optimism after the war in what might be termed "progressive evolution," a combination of post-Darwinian thought and Hegelian idealism. Whitman declared, "Only Hegel is fit for America—is large enough and free enough."[30] Hegel's formula of thesis-antithesis-synthesis brought great consolation to him, because it suggested that, no matter what, things would work out in time. All the social ills of modern America, he now believed, would be resolved by "a native expression-spirit" of "original authors and poets to come."[31]

His religious inclinations gathered strength after the war. In outlining "the future personality of America" in "Democratic Vistas," he said that a "primary moral element," a "sane and pervasive religiousness" must be developed. His postbellum writings often turned to what he saw as the soul's voyage to other spheres. For example, his 1871 poem "Passage to India" begins by singing praise to the modern inventions, then predicts the coming of a future poet, "the true son of God" who "shall come singing his songs," and ends by declaring, "Away O soul!," in a rapturous vision of the flight of the soul through the harmonious universe.[32] Similarly, in "Gliding O'er All" he envisages "the voyage of the soul—not life alone, / Death, many deaths, I'll sing."

If his poetry had become more spiritual, it also became more traditional in its relation to America. In the fifties, his collapsed belief in the party system and presidential power had caused an incredible surge of his omnivorous, all-gathering poetic "I," creating his richest poetry. After the war, in the wake of Lincoln, his "I" was in retreat. He looked to the electoral process and American presidents to resolve social problems on a large scale.

Despite his growing political conservatism, Whitman remained devoted to the radical poetic project he had initiated in 1855. True, the postbellum editions of *Leaves of Grass* were in some senses more conventional than the early editions. Some of the most radical poems, especially "Respondez!," were toned down. The diction became more formal (e.g., "thee" and "thou" sometimes replaced "you"), and the punctuation more normal (e.g., commas and periods replaced ellipses). Nonetheless, most of the poems of the fifties remained intact, with slight revision. To the end, Whitman dreamed that his volume would be appreciated by what he called "myriads of readers."[33]

His dream has come true. Since his death he has earned a secure place in the literary pantheon. No writer is regarded as more indisputably American than he, yet no one has reverberated on the international scene to the extent he has. His liberation of the poetic line from formal rhythm and rhyme was a landmark event with which all poets since have had to come to terms with. His equally bold treatment of erotic themes has provided a fertile field for interpretation and has contributed to the candid discussion of sex in the larger culture. The radically egalitarian nature of his poems consistently inspired progressives of all stripes. His boundless love and all-inclusive language, reflected in his extraordinary intimacy with his contemporary culture, makes his writing attractive for practically all readers.

At his best, he was the democratic poet to an extent never matched, gathering images from virtually every cultural arena and transforming them through his powerful personality into art. By fully absorbing his time, he became a writer for all times.

Whitman in 1891, the year before his death.
Ed Folsom Collection

ABBREVIATIONS

BE   *Brooklyn Daily Eagle*

CG   Whitman, Walt. *Walt Whitman and the Civil War: A Collection of original articles and manuscripts*. Edited by Charles Glicksberg. Philadelphia: University of Pennsylvania Press, 1933.

CWW   *Complete Writings of Walt Whitman*. Edited by T. B. Harned, R. M. Bucke, and Horace Traubel. New York: G. P. Putnam's Sons, 1902.

DN   Whitman, Walt. *Daybooks and Notebooks*. Edited by William White. 3 vols. New York: New York University Press, 1978. Vol. I: 1876–Nov. 1881. Vol. II: 1881–1891. Vol. III: *Diary in Canada, Notebooks*.

FC   *Faint Clews & Indirections: Manuscripts of Walt Whitman and His Family*. Edited by Clarence Gohdes and Rollo G. Silver. Durham, NC: Duke University Press, 1949.

GF   *The Gathering of the Forces*. Edited by Cleveland Rodgers and John Black. 2 vols. New York: G. P. Putnam's Sons, 1920.

H   *Walt Whitman, the Critical Heritage*. Edited by Milton Hindus. New York: Barnes & Noble, 1971.

InRe   *In Re Walt Whitman*. Edited by Horace L. Traubel, R. M. Bucke, and Thomas B. Harned. Philadelphia: David McKay, 1893.

ISit   Whitman, Walt. *I Sit and Look Out: Editorials from the Brooklyn Daily Times*. Edited by Emory Holloway and Vernolian Schwartz. New York: AMS Press, 1966.

LGC   Whitman, Walt. *Leaves of Grass, Comprehensive Reader's Edition*. Edited by Harold Blodgett and Sculley Bradley. New York: New York University Press, 1965.

LV   Whitman, Walt. *Leaves of Grass, A Textual Variorum of the Printed Poems.* Edited by Sculley Bradley, Harold W. Blodgett, Arthur Golden, and William White. New York: New York University Press, 1980. Vol. I: 1855–1856. Vol. II: 1860–1867. Vol. III: 1870–1891.

NF   Whitman, Walt. *Notes and Fragments.* Edited by R. M. Bucke. 1899. Reprint, Ontario: A. Talbot and Co., n.d.

NUPM   Whitman, Walt. *Notebooks and Unpublished Prose Manuscripts.* Edited by Edward H. Grier. 6 vols. New York: New York University Press, 1984.

PW   Whitman, Walt. *Prose Works, 1892.* Edited by Floyd Stovall. 2 vols. New York: New York University Press. Vol. I: *Specimen Days* (1963). Vol. II: *Collect and Other Prose* (1964).

UPP   *The Uncollected Prose and Poetry of Walt Whitman.* Edited by Emory Holloway. 2 vols. Gloucester, MA: Peter Smith, 1972.

WCP   Whitman, Walt. *Complete Poetry and Collected Prose.* New York: Library of America, 1982.

WEP   Whitman, Walt. *The Early Poems and the Fiction.* Edited by Thomas L. Brasher. New York: New York University Press, 1963.

WWC   Traubel, Horace. *With Walt Whitman in Camden.* 7 vols. Vols. I, II, III originally published in 1905, 1907, and 1912, respectively; all three reprinted by Rowman and Littlefield (New York) 1961. Vols. IV–VII published in 1953, 1964, 1982, and 1992, respectively, by Southern Illinois University Press (Carbondale).

NOTES

NOTES TO PREFACE

1. *WCP* 1326.
2. *WWC* 2:430. The next quotation in this paragraph is in 1:167.
3. *PW* 2:473.
4. *LGC* 344.

NOTES TO CHAPTER ONE

1. *WCP* 492.
2. *InRe* 34.
3. *WCP* 492.
4. *WCP* 698.
5. *WWC* 3:205.
6. *UPP* 1: xxvi, n. 9.
7. *WWC* 1:194, 2:480.
8. Scudder Whitney to Lotta Rees, letter of August 18, 1906; Walt Whitman Birthplace Association Library, Huntington, New York.
9. See Arthur Golden, "Nine Early Whitman Letters, 1840–1841," *American Literature* 58 (October 1986): 342–60.
10. *WCP* 188.
11. *WWC* 2:283.
12. *WCP* 548
13. *InRe* 33.
14. *PW* 1:473.
15. *WCP* 23.
16. J. T. Trowbridge, "Reminiscences of Walt Whitman," *Atlantic Monthly* 89 (February 1902):166.
17. *LGC* 729.
18. *WCP* 660.
19. *WCP* 40, 57.
20. *WCP* 1326. The next quotation in this paragraph is also on p. 1326.

21. *H* 34.
22. *H* 32, 61.
23. *WCP* 26.
24. *NUPM* 1:167.
25. *WCP* 311.
26. *LV* 1:262.
27. *WCP* 478.
28. *WCP* 1327.
29. *NUPM* 4:1554.
30. William Thayer and Charles Eldridge to Walt Whitman, letter of February 10, 1860; Charles E. Feinberg Collection, Library of Congress.
31. *Leaves of Grass Imprints* (Boston: Thayer and Eldridge, 1860), back jacket.
32. *FC* 215.
33. *WCP* 988.

NOTES TO CHAPTER TWO

1. *Whitman in His Own Time*, ed. Joel Myerson (Detroit: Omnigraphics, 1991), p. 43
2. *LGC* 657.
3. *WEP* 127.
4. *WWC* 1:93.
5. *WCP* 408. The next quotation in this paragraph is on p. 303.
6. *WEP* 10.
7. *UPP* 2:20–1.
8. See *WCP* 226–29.
9. *NYD* 140.
10. *Brooklyn Daily Advertiser*, June 28, 1851.
11. *Brooklyn Evening Star*, May 21, 1846.
12. *WCP* 312. The next quotation in this paragraph is also on p. 312. The quotations in the next two paragraphs are on pp. 195, 613, 585–86, and 210, respectively.
13. *WCP* 1190.
14. *DN* 3:669, 736.
15. *WCP* 242–43.
16. *New York Examiner*, January 19, 1882.
17. *ISit* 43.
18. *Brooklyn Daily Times*, February 20, 1858.
19. *WCP* 479 and *LV* 1: 188–89.
20. *H* 22.

21. *H* 22.
22. *Life Illustrated*, July 28, 1855.
23. Boston *Transcript*, July 3, 1888.
24. *H* 25.
25. *WCP* 50.
26. *WCP* 8.
27. *WWC* 5:529.
28. *WCP* 9.
29. *WCP* 470 and *WCP* 379.
30. *LGC* 296. The block quotation after the next sentence is on p. 77.
31. *WCP* 18. The quotations in the next two paragraphs are on pp. 1317, 1313, 706, and 1310, respectively.
32. *WWC* 1:223. The next quotation in this paragraph is in 1:166.
33. *Brooklyn Daily Eagle*, February 23, 1847.
34. *UPP* 1:194.
35. *WCP* 1320. The next quotation in this paragraph is on p. 1318.
36. *NUPM* 1:69.
37. *Brooklyn Daily Eagle*, August 26, 1846.
38. *WCP* 1008.
39. *WCP* 9. The quotations in the next six paragraphs are on pp. 9, 8, 6, 18, 27, 188, 193, 203–4, 15, 8, 320, 225, and 256, respectively.
40. *Walt Whitman: The Measure of His Song*, eds. Jim Perlman, Ed Folsom, and Dan Campion (Minneapolis: Holy Cow! Press, 1981), pp. 96 and 351.

NOTES TO CHAPTER THREE
1. *WWC* 1:455.
2. *WCP* 1189. The quotations in the next paragraph are on pp. 1192 and 1187, respectively.
3. *WWC* 4:141.
4. *WCP* 1192.
5. *WWC* 7:295.
6. *CG* 56.
7. *WWC* 4:519.
8. *Whitman in His Own Time*, ed. J. Myerson, p. 33.
9. Quoted in David S. Reynolds, *Walt Whitman's America: A Cultural Biography* (New York: Alfred A. Knopf, 1995), p. 161.
10. *WCP* 508.
11. *LGC* 67 and *LV* 1:59
12. *WCP* 544. The next quotation in this paragraph is on p. 313.

13. *LV* 1: 58, *LGC* 71, and *WCP* 216.
14. *WWC* 6:457.
15. W. Whitman, "Democracy" (1867), in *Democratic Vistas, 1860–1880*, ed. Alan Trachtenberg (New York: George Braziller, 1970), p. 359.
16. *Brooklyn Daily Times*, January 30, 1857.
17. *NUPM* 6:2230.
18. *LV* 1:83–84.
19. *WWC* 1:5.
20. *NUPM* 1:314.
21. *NUPM* 6: 2232. The next quotation in this paragraph is on p. 2236.
22. *WWC* 2:26–27. The next quotation in this paragraph is in *WWC* 3:375.
23. *WCP* 327.
24. See especially C. Caroll Hollis, *Language and Style in* Leaves of Grass (Baton Rouge: Louisiana State University Press, 1983) and Christopher Charles Burnam, "An Analysis and Description of Walt Whitman's Composing Process" (Ph.D. diss., University of Rhode Island, 1979).
25. Quoted in Harold Blodgett, *Walt Whitman in England* (1934; New York: Russell & Russell, 1973), p. 21.
26. *PW* 2:725.
27. *WCP* 992. The next quotation in this paragraph is on p. 611.
28. *PW* 2:592.
29. *WWC* 2:174.
30. Statistics from Robert D. Faner, *Walt Whitman and the Opera* (Carbondale: Southern Illinois University Press, 1951), p. 122.
31. *WCP* 6.
32. *ISit* 173.
33. *Brooklyn Star*, November 5, 1845.
34. *NF* 70.
35. *GF* 346.
36. *WCP* 564.
37. *WWC* 6:120.
38. R. Faner, *Whitman and the Opera*, p. 63.
39. C. Hamm, *Music in the New World* (New York: W. W. Norton, 1973), p. 231.
40. *WCP* 174.
41. *WWC* 2:173.
42. *WCP* 215. The next quotation in this paragraph is on p. 625.
43. *WCP* 625.
44. *WWC* 4:286.
45. George C. D. Odell, *Annals of the New York Stage* (New York: Columbia University Press, 1928), 6:187.

46. *PW* 1:20.
47. J. Johnston and J. W. Wallace, *Visits to Walt Whitman in 1890–1891* (London: G. Allen & Unwin, 1912), p. 162.
48. G. C. D. Odell, *Annals*, 6:264.
49. *WCP* 208. The next two quotations are on pp. 215 and 528.
50. *FC* 19.
51. *UPP* I: 98.
52. *Saturday Press*, January 7, 1860, and J. T. Trowbridge, "Reminiscences of Walt Whitman," p. 166.
53. *WCP* 640.

NOTES TO CHAPTER FOUR
1. *Brooklyn Daily Eagle*, March 12, 1846.
2. *NUPM* 4:1524.
3. *LGC* 642.
4. *WWC* 4:125.
5. *LV* 1: 92, 18.
6. *GF* 2: 114–15.
7. *Brooklyn Star*, February 2, 1846.
8. *Walt Whitman and the Visual Arts*, eds. Geoffrey M. Sill and Roberta M. Tarbell (New Brunswick: Rutgers University Press, 1992), pp. 6–7.
9. *WWC* 1:131.
10. *WCP* 236.
11. *Form and Function: Remarks on Art by Horatio Greenough*, ed. Harold A. Small (Berkeley: University of California Press, 1947), pp. xvi, 120.
12. *WCP* 19. The next quotation in this paragraph is on p. 11.
13. *LGC* 30.
14. See *WCP* 196–97.
15. *UPP* 1:238.
16. *WCP* 198–99.
17. Burroughs, *Walt Whitman, A Study* (1896; New York: AMS, 1969), p. 143.
18. *LGC* 42–43. The quotations in the next paragraph are on pp. 42 and 203, respectively.
19. *Brooklyn Daily Eagle*, November 18, 1847, and April 14, 1847.
20. *WCP* 632. The quotation from "To You" in the paragraph after the next one is on p. 376.
21. *PW* 1:268.
22. *WWC* 2:407. The next quotation in this paragraph is in 1:7.
23. *UPP* 1:298.
24. *LGC* 430.

25. *UPP* 1:246.

26. *ISit* 129–30.

27. *PW* 2:681.

28. *The World of Science, Art, and Industry Illustrated from Examples in the New-York Exhibition, 1853–54,* eds. B. Silliman and C. R. Goodrich (New York: G. P. Putnam, 1854), p. 15.

29. *LV* 1:92.

30. *LGC* 642–43.

NOTES TO CHAPTER FIVE

1. *WCP* 369. The quotations in the next three paragraphs are on pp. 236, 383, and 1332, respectively.

2. *LV* 1:262.

3. *LGC* 434–35.

4. *LV* 1:25.

5. *WCP* 237.

6. *Brooklyn Daily Eagle,* June 28, 1847.

7. J. Liebig, *Organic Chemistry in Its Application to Agriculture and Physiology* (London: Taylor and Walton, 1840), p. 225.

8. *LGC* 107–8.

9. *WCP* 193, 194, and 245.

10. J. Liebig, *Organic Chemistry,* p. 336.

11. *WCP* 495. The next quotation is on p. 496.

12. *WCP* 310.

13. *LGC* 439.

14. *WCP* 240. The next five quotations are on pp. 245, 239, 50, 210, and 516–17, respectively.

15. *Brooklyn Daily Eagle,* March 10, 1846.

16. Madeleine B. Stern, *Heads and Headlines: The Phrenological Fowlers* (Norman, OK: University of Oklahoma Press, 1971), p. 102.

17. *WWC* 1:385.

18. *WCP* 15, 20.

19. *LV* 1:189.

20. *WCP* 251.

21. Orson S. Fowler, *Amativeness, or, Evils and Remedies of Excessive and Perverted Sexuality* (New York: Fowler & Wells, 1846), p. 56.

22. *NUPM* 1:438.

23. O. S. Fowler, *Fowler on Matrimony: or, the Principles of Phrenology and Physiology Applied to the Selection of Suitable Companions for Life* (Philadelphia: n. p, 1841), p. 5.

24. *NUPM* 2:888–90.

25. *NUPM* 1:886–87.

26. *WCP* 210. The first quotation in the next paragraph is on pp. 1002–3.

27. *PW* 2:365.

28. *WWC* 2:149.

29. *Whitman in His Own Time*, ed. J. Myerson, p. 30.

30. *WWC* 4:239.

31. Lavater, in Frederic H. Hedge, *Prose Writers of Germany* (Philadelphia: Porter & Coates, 1847), p. 191.

32. *WCP* 237. The next quotation in this paragraph is on p. 1143.

33. *NUPM* 6:2043.

34. *WWC* 1:138.

35. *WCP* 245.

36. *WWC* 2:457.

37. *WCP* 233–34. The next quotations in this paragraph are on pp. 9 and 11, respectively.

38. *NUPM* 1:353.

39. *LGC* 20.

40. Henry David Thoreau, *Correspondence*, eds. Walter Harding and Carl Bode (New York: New York University Press, 1958), p. 445.

41. *New York Sunday Times*, August 14, 1842.

42. Dods, *The Philosophy of Electrical Psychology* (New York: Fowlers & Wells, 1850), p. 61 .

43. *WCP* 215. The next quotation is on p. 250.

44. *Brooklyn Daily Times*, June 26, 1857.

45. *WCP* 15.

46. *LGC* 48.

47. *InRe* 19.

48. *LGC* 481.

49. *WCP* 590.

50. *LGC* 602 and *WCP* 263.

51. *WCP* 595.

52. *UPP* 2:16. The first quotation in the next paragraph is in 2:18.

53. *LGC* 23.

54. *WCP* 313. The two quotations in the next paragraph are on pp. 301 and 302.

55. *WCP* 301. The following quotation in this paragraph is on p. 302.

56. *WWC* 5:376.

57. *WCP* 192. The next quotation in this paragraph is also on p. 192.

58. *NUPM* 1:194.

59. *Walt Whitman's Workshop: A Collection of Unpublished Prose Manucsripts*, ed.Clifton Joseph Furness (New York: Russell & Russell, 1964), p. 191.

60. *WCP* 219. The next quotation in this paragraph is on p. 223. The quotations in the following three paragraphs are on pp. 208, 213, and 247, successively.

61. *Saturday Press*, June 30, 1860.

62. London *Critic*, 15 (April 1, 1856):171.

63. *H* 84.

NOTES TO CHAPTER SIX

1. *NUPM* 4:1604.

2. *WCP* 975.

3. *WWC* 4:119. The next quotation in this paragraph in 4:388.

4. *UPP* 1:122.

5. *Brooklyn Daily Times*, August 17, 1857.

6. W. D. O'Connor, *The Good Gray Poet* (1866; reprint in Richard Maurice Bucke, *Walt Whitman* [New York: Johnson Reprint Corporation, 1970]), p. 108.

7. J. Burroughs, *Notes on Walt Whitman, as Poet and Person* (1867; New York: Haskell House, 1971), 27.

8. *NUPM* 1:413.

9. *PW* 2:767.

10. *WCP* 19. The quoted poem in the next paragraph is on pp. 346–47.

11. Orson S. Fowler and Lorenzo N. Fowler, *Marriage: Its History and Ceremonies* (New York: Fowlers & Wells, 1847), p. 229.

12. O. S. Fowler, *Sexual Science; Including Manhood, Womanhood, and Their Mutual Interrelations* (Philadelphia: National Publishing Co., 1870), p. 638.

13. *WCP* 259.

14. *WWC* 3:452.

15. O. S. Fowler, *Sexual Science*, p. 712.

16. *WWC* 2:148.

17. *UPP* 1:191.

18. *WCP* 19. The next quotation in this paragraph is on p. 19.

19. *NUPM* 1:304.

20. *ISit* 113.

21. *WCP* 19. The next quotation in this paragraph is on p. 190.

22. *LGC* 432.

23. *WWC* 4:386.

24. *LGC* 1.

25. *NF* 33.

26. Quoted in D. S. Reynolds, *Walt Whitman's America: A Cultural Biography*, (New York: Knopf, 1995), p. 215.

27. *LGC* 97.

28. *WCP* 515–16. The quotation in the paragraph after the next is on p. 259.

29. *WWC* 2:331.

30. *WCP* 336.

31. Florence Bernstein Freedman, *William Douglas O'Connor: Walt Whitman's Chosen Knight* (Athens: Ohio University Press, 1985), p. 169.

32. *ISit* 113–14.

33. *WCP* 312. The next quotation in this paragraph is on p. 330. The quotation in the next paragraph is on p. 265.

34. NYD 217. The quotations in the next paragraph are on pp. 119–20.

35. O. S. Fowler, *Love and Parentage: Applied to the Improvement of Offspring* (New York: Fowler & Wells, 1844), p. 98.

36. *WCP* 411. The next quotation in this paragraph is on p. 202. The quoted poem in the next paragraph is on p. 512.

37. *WCP* 207. The quotation in the paragraph after the next is on p. 356.

38. *NUPM* 3:976.

39. *WCP* 259.

40. Ralph Waldo Emerson, *Essays and Lectures* (New York: Library of America, 1983), p. 343.

41. *LV* 2:381.

42. *WCP* 279. The quotation in the next paragraph is also on p. 279.

43. *DN* 3: 740–41.

44. *WCP* 1335.

45. O. Fowler, *Phrenology Proved, Illustrated and Accompanied by a Chart* (New York: Fowlers & Wells, 1842), p. 65. The next quotation in this paragraph is also on p. 65.

46. *NUPM* 1:412, 413.

47. *WCP* 610. The next quotation in this paragraph is on p. 274.

48. *WWC* 6: 342–43.

49. *WCP* 1011.

50. *LV* 2:371–72.

51. *WCP* 272.

NOTES TO CHAPTER SEVEN

1. *LGC* 4.

2. *PW* 2:469.

3. *WCP* 994–96. The quotation in the next paragraph is on p. 418.

4. *LGC* 66.

5. *LGC* 281.

6. *WCP* 419.

7. *WCP* 778.

8. *LGC* 317–18.

9. *WCP* 444.

10. W. Whitman, *The Correspondence. Vol. I: 1842–67*, ed. Edwin Haviland Miller (New York: New York University Press, 1961), p. 69.

11. *WWC* 6:194–95.

12. *PW* 1:65.

13. *WCP* 438.

14. *PW* 1:312.

15. *WCP* 763. The first quotation in the next paragraph is on p. 732–33.

16. W. Whitman, *The Correspondence. Vol. I: 1842–67*, p. 82.

17. *PW* 2:603–5.

18. *PW* 2:602–3.

19. *PW* 1:98.

20. *PW* 2:508.

21. *WCP* 459–60.

22. *Memoranda During the War & Death of President Lincoln*, ed. Roy P. Basler (Bloomington: Indiana University Press, 1962), p. 4.

23. *WWC* 6:147.

24. *WCP* 1050–51.

25. *WCP* 165. The quotation in the next paragraph is on p. 824.

26. *PW* 2:762.

27. *WWC* 2:283.

28. John S. Haller, Jr., *Outcasts from Evolution: Scientific Attitudes about Racial Inferiority, 1859–1900* (Urbana: University of Illinois Press, 1971) p. 324.

29. *PW* 2: 369–70.

30. *NUPM* 6:2011.

31. *PW* 2:410. The first quotation in the next paragraph is in 2:397–98.

32. *WCP* 534, 539. The next quotation in this paragraph is on p. 414.

33. *LGC* 544.

Notes on Further Reading

The definitive edition of Whitman's writings is *The Collected Writings of Walt Whitman*, published by the New York University Press. This wonderful multivolume edition contains all of Whitman's poetry and much of his prose.

Selections of Whitman's journalism can be found in *The Journalism: 1834–1846. Vol. I*, edited by Herbert Bergman, Douglas A. Noverr, and Edward J. Recchia (New York: Peter Lang, 1998); *The Gathering of the Forces*, edited by Cleveland Rodgers and John Black (New York: G. P. Putnam's, 1920); and *I Sit and Look Out: Editorials from the Brooklyn Daily Times,* edited by Emory Holloway and Vernolian Schwartz (New York: AMS, 1966). The lively conversations the poet had late in life with his young follower Horace Traubel are recorded in the seven-volume *With Walt Whitman in Camden*.

For a broad range of Whitman's writings and selected commentary by leading critics, see the Second Edition of the *Norton Critical Edition of Whitman*, edited by Michael Moon, Sculley Bradley, and Harold Blodgett (New York: W. W. Norton, 2002). Also extremely useful is the *Complete Poetry and Collected Prose*, edited by Justin Kaplan (New York: Library of America, 1982), which contains both the 1855 and 1892 editions of *Leaves of Grass,* along with a rich sampling of the prose writings.

Some fifteen biographies of Whitman have appeared. Gay Wilson Allen's *The Solitary Singer*, first published in 1955 and revised in 1985 (Chicago: University of Chicago Press) is a judicious overview of the poet's life. Paul Zweig's *Walt Whitman: The Making of the Poet* (New York: Basic, 1984) is a sensitive treatment of the acme of Whitman's career, in the 1840s and 1850s. A thorough recent biography is Jerome Loving's *Walt Whitman: The Song of Himself* (Berkeley: University of California Press, 1999). David S. Reynolds's *Walt Whitman's America: A Cultural Biography* (New York: Knopf, 1986) recounts the poet's life in the context of the cultural, political, and social forces that shaped him.

There have been a number of fine studies of Whitman and individual historical or cultural phenomena. Some highlights: Betsy Erkkila's *Whitman: The*

Political Poet (New York: Oxford University Press, 1989); Shelley Fisher Fishkin's *From Fact to Fiction: Journalism and Imaginative Writing in America* (Baltimore: Johns Hopkins University Press, 1985); David Kuebrich's *Minor Prophecy: Walt Whitman's New American Religion* (Bloomington: Indiana University Press, 1989); George Hutchinson's *The Ecstatic Whitman* (Columbus: Ohio State University Press, 1985); Robert Leigh Davis's *Whitman and the Romance of Medicine* (Berkeley: University of California Press, 1997); C. Caroll Hollis's *Language and Style in "Leaves of Grass"* (Baton Rouge: Louisiana State University Press, 1983); Ezra Greenspan's *Walt Whitman and the American Reader* (New York: Cambridge University Press, 1990); James Perrin Warren's *Walt Whitman's Language Experiment* (University Park: Pennsylvania State University Press, 1987); Martin Klammer's *Whitman, Slavery, and the Emergence of "Leaves of Grass"* (University Park: Pennsylvania State University Press, 1995); Luke Mancuso's *The Strange Sad War Revolving: Walt Whitman, Reconstruction, and the Emergence of Black Citizenship, 1865–1876* (Columbia, SC: Camden House, 1997). Ed Folsom's *Walt Whitman's Native Representations* (New York: Cambridge University Press, 1994) considers the poet in relation to photography, baseball, and American Indian culture.

Explorations of gender issues, eroticism, and homosexuality in Whitman include Michael Moon's *Disseminating Whitman: Revision and Corporeality in "Leaves of Grass"* (Cambridge, MA: Harvard University Press, 1991); Byrne R. S. Fone's *Masculine Landscapes: Walt Whitman and the Homoerotic Text* (Carbondale: Southern Illinois University Press, 1992); Robert K. Martin's *The Homosexual Tradition in American Poetry* (Austin: University of Texas Press, 1979); Gary Schmidgall's *Walt Whitman: A Gay Life* (New York: Dutton, 1997); M. Jimmie Killingsworth's *Whitman's Poetry of the Body* (Chapel Hill: University of North Carolina Press, 1989); and *Calamus Lovers: Walt Whitman's Working-Class Camerados*, edited by Charley Shiveley (San Francisco: Gay Sunshine, 1987).

A comprehensive compendium of analyses of many aspects of the poet's life and work is *The Walt Whitman Encyclopedia*, edited by J. R. Lemaster and Donald D. Kummings (New York: Garland, 1998).

Studies of Whitman's influence include Robert K. Martin's *The Continuing Presence of Walt Whitman* (Iowa City: University of Iowa Press, 1992) and *Walt Whitman: The Measure of His Song*, edited by Jim Perlman, Ed Folsom, and Dan Campion (Duluth: Holy Cow! Press, 1998).

Index

Whitman, Walter (father of WW), 3–4

Whitman, Zechariah, 1

Whittier, John Greenleaf, 14

Wilde, Oscar, 22

Wright, Fanny, 5, 110